POETRY

now

The Power Of Words

Edited by

Sarah Marshall

First published in Great Britain in 2004 by
POETRY NOW
Remus House,
Coltsfoot Drive,
Peterborough, PE2 9JX
Telephone (01733) 898101
Fax (01733) 313524

SB ISBN 1 84460 851 4

FOREWORD

Although we are a nation of poets we are accused of not reading poetry, or buying poetry books. After many years of listening to the incessant gripes of poetry publishers, I can only assume that the books they publish, in general, are books that most people do not want to read.

Poetry should not be obscure, introverted, and as cryptic as a crossword puzzle: it is the poet's duty to reach out and embrace the world.

The world owes the poet nothing and we should not be expected to dig and delve into a rambling discourse searching for some inner meaning.

The reason we write poetry (and almost all of us do) is because we want to communicate: an ideal; an idea; or a specific feeling. Poetry is as essential in communication, as a letter; a radio; a telephone, and the main criterion for selecting the poems in this anthology is very simple: they communicate.

Contents

PRINCIPLE

Where is he now I wonder
Does he ever think of me
We had our chance so long ago
But only one of us was free

I thought of him, of course I did
Couldn't get him off my mind
I had to make a phone call
Leaving my principles behind

Yet each time I came to call him
His children I could see
He was going to leave them
Start a brand new life with me

But my conscience wouldn't let me
My own happiness at stake
It's only now when I look back
It was such a big mistake

I'd sacrificed a love
I'd never felt before
That it could have worked
I'll never know for sure

Lynne Taylor

The Grim Reaper

His robe was coarse and tawny, brown sandals on his feet;
A cowl and hood hid his face, his work was swift and neat.

He stood amid this field of corn, a scythe he swung with care;
A giant scythe of burnished steel, just whistled thro' the air.

And as each stroke was wielded, the edge was honed and keen
You couldn't see a footprint where the man had been.

Then suddenly I realised, I was in this field:
Standing straight (a stalk of corn), was I part of the yield?

As the man grew nearer, his scythe still cutting corn:
I saw his face beneath the hood, a bony mask of scorn.

No colour in his fleshless skull, black sockets for his eyes;
Teeth set in an evil grin, as he swung his mighty scythe.

I saw him really close to me and fear just filled my breast;
I knew this figure from my dreams and his unending quest.

He swung his scythe. I shouted, 'No, my time has not yet come,'
The Reaper stopped his downward stroke, fear had struck me dumb.

Then I spoke again, 'Please spare me stop your grisly reap;
I have lots of things to do and promises to keep.'

'This field is due for cutting, of this harvest, you are part;
I cannot leave you standing, there are other fields to start.

You've had your chance, this lifetime and now your time is due,
When all the stalks have withered, life will start anew.'

With that, the scythe completed its awful whistling stroke;
And as it sought to end my life, I suddenly awoke.

Of course I had been dreaming, the Reaper, grim no more!
But I was so afraid of him I just sat on the floor.

I thought so long and hard that day, of war and worldwide strife;
Of promises I'd made, not kept, I'd really change my life.

For who knows how much time is left in life's mysterious dance;
To stay the Reaper's scythe, you might not get the chance.

Brian Bates

SECRET GARDEN

Music playing in the background, melodious and sweet,
the same sweet harmony that death clings to
when it tricks you into defeat.
Oh sweet music, cancel thy harmonious tune,
take it and throw it in the well for death will have thee soon.
The doves are watching over as the maiden dances slow,
the harmony of death that has a sickly glow.
A drop of blood is listening to thy heartbeat as it pounds,
a million senses wandering and falling to the ground.
I take thee to the gardens where the dancing always goes,
I dance with thee and lavender upon an ebony rose.
Enchantment rises in this furrow, wallowing in the sun,
upon this eve of autumn time the uprising has begun.
I make nothing of this haunted eve of love
and whisper in the corner to the ever listening dove,
Fly away my soulless friend, into the oncoming light
and wallow the goodness that passes through as
daytime turns to night.
The music stops and the dove will fall
the girl still dancing floats through the wall,
A spirit of Eve is watching us all
and cloaked in white she stops no more.
Still dancing as she passes through
what once was white is now blue,
Time is rushing through the plain
and the music begins once again.
Like an eternity washing past
sweet music dies and never lasts,
Entrapped inside the garden walls,
the girl stops dancing and the dove will fall.

Barbara Scott

THE ORPHAN'S CRY

It has not been long since she went away,
There is no smile - only yesterday.
My feet are cold on the polished floor,
The floor which I polished only yesterday.
The same thing day after day.
I wish she was here - I miss her so.

Maybe tomorrow,
I cry my tears
And dry them quickly
In case someone's near!
They're not allowed - not here!
Down to breakfast
My age is three,
I wish my mummy was here
Who are these people?
Where is she?
She will come back, she loves me,
I cling to a hand, that is not mine.
Oh how I wish I was at home in her big bed.
I cry! I cry!
But they cannot hear the orphan cry!
Oh! How I wish! They could hear the orphan's cry!

Evelyn Riverside

The Naughty Monkey

There's a monkey
In my house
He's painted green
With his hands on his mouth.

I don't know his secret
But it's making him feel bad
He can't sleep
And he looks very sad.

I'm afraid he'll pop
If he doesn't let it out
And tell someone
What this is about.

Me and my brothers
Once lived in a store
High in a window
Close to the door

Down below on a table
Stood General Napier
With his friend Juliet
And a handsome dog pair.

Our lady was dusting
The swan on the floor
When Miranda, the mermaid
Grew jealous and sore

With a thrash of her tail
She upset a vase
And the wild pony on it
Kicked the bookcase

Thor, who was sleeping
Awoke with a jolt
Then away flew his hammer
Like a big thunderbolt
The wall began shaking
And to our lady's dismay
I jumped from the top shelf
Right into the 'fray

Imagine her surprise to see
A broken monkey at her feet
She didn't want to pay for me
She had a little boy to feed
Still I went home in a sack
Where she carefully glued
My pieces back.

I wish that I could tell her
But I don't know what to say
When the truth is . . .
I'm a naughty monkey
Who had to have his way.

Juliet Tune

Suicidal

I'm wondering just how to do it
I've been turning first this way then that
I'd jump from the town's tallest building
But I can't bear the thought of the splat!

To drown in the river's not easy
It's not safe with old pushchairs and bikes
A bedhead or two and a rake half sawn through
I might get caught up on the spikes.

Jump in front of a train, that's the answer
But the Porter has just been to say
Due to a blanket of fog down in Bletchley
No trains will be running today.

Gin and aspirin didn't work either
The bottle of gin tasted grand
But when I awoke hours later
The tablets were still in my hand.

So I guess I'm just not meant to do it
I'll have to give in and survive
Tea and toast coming up, where's the kettle?
It's my favourite time, around five.

Paula Holland

The Hands Of Time

The hands of time that move so fast
When all around is changing fast
The future, they're of things to come
And memories of days that's done

There in the past the memories keep
The morning after a good night's sleep
The joys and pain, we all must share
As we go through each coming year.

Now to the future we must turn
Of things to come, new things to learn
A new awakening there each day
Will greet us in our work and play.

There to the people we must say
Look out for those that come your way
Be kind and helpful as you can
For after all, you're just a man.

R Claxton

A Scream Of Disgust

What Have We Brits Become?

We have the worst hospitals in the world, full of killer bugs. MRSA.
UK has the worst roads where huge holes suddenly appear
and the streets are full of rubbish.
No wonder we have rats as big as cats, ten for every man and woman
in the cities so I'm told.

We have the worst crime rate, where the weak and old folk get robbed
of their pensions and belongings and all the robbers get is a
slap on the hand.

The worst so-called businesses where we all get ripped off
by the plumbers from Hell, the roofers from Hell and the
computer programmers from Hell.
Also the butchers from Hell where they cut your freshly cooked meat
with a knife full of blood from dead animals.

Old folk who are paid less than the Asylum Seekers who come
to England to look for a better life - and with ten wives!

The worst government in the world where honesty is not the
best policy.
The worst supermarkets who charge the most for the latest.
Oh! What a lovely way to run a land with no shame in hand -
Why don't we shake your hand?
For the worst run land in the world.

Now when will our government wake up?
You're only in the job you hold because the people put you there
and that's to run this land for the people and *not yourselves!*
To serve the people is your task and that clearly you cannot do!

The rot set in very soon after the second world war.
What Hitler was trying to do, by force
you are doing by your hand.

No more motorcycles are British; no more cars are British,
No more coal or steel are British, and where is the fine British porcelain ? Gone just like all the rest!
And now not even the streets are cleaned.

Give Northern Ireland back to the Irish and Iraq back to the Iraqis
So that we can live in peace
And leave the bloody wars to the Yanks!

Paul Volante

REMEMBER SEPTEMBER

Let this be the time when we remember
the eleventh of September.
How it spawned a world of terror for all.
To understand the human psyche of hate,
when violence dares to call itself Holy.
When politicians gathered and armies assembled
the machines of war.
And young men died in boots so strong
and those in sandals worn
And hearts were torn.
Let this be the time when history's lessons
are thought not hollow,
by those who lead and those who follow.
Uncurl their fists of vengeful hate,
and steadfast steps to peace they take.

Fae Turner

HOPPERS WOOD

Blue-tipped, they
Spear their way through musty earth
While stars, white and trembling
Gather at their feet

For now, no joyous peal,
Their full-blown glory
Yet to be

Red-blushed, he
Sings his way through choral glee
Declaring boundaries old
Instinctively complete

For now, content to wait
Hopeful promise
Yet to be

Sage-edged with
Fingers stretched to warming sky
While under dampened ground
Root and reason meet

For now, soft swollen buds
Shaded canopy
Yet to be

Rose-tinged, my
Earthly worries calmed and stilled
In wondrous silent awe
Senses soar replete

For now, suspended time,
Loved memories
Yet to be

Sue Percival

VIRUS

I'm infected, firewall breached,
I could no longer stay the siege,
Your program in,
It's multiplying,
My system swamped, my interface engulfed,

My software offered no protection,
No hope of halt despite detection,
My network open
To all you've spoken,
My drivers drowned, my memory overflowing, yet . . .

My unit seeks no consolation,
Instead it wallows in virtual salvation,
This conscious thought
Your invasion brought,
Connection established, I surf the waves.

Tom Peacock

HEAVENLY FATHER

Heavenly Father up above
I want to send my mum our love.
She came to You, no suffering or pain
but in our hearts she will remain.

You came along, You took her hand
and took her to Your heavenly land.
I know you couldn't stay because your days were done
But I want you to know, we miss you Mum

Now Dean is seven, he misses you so much
your gentle smile, your tender touch.
He looks up at the sky at night
and says you're the star that shines so bright.

So at night he says, 'Goodnight, God bless,'
so now it's time Gran, for you to rest.
So dear God, please hear my plea
and please look after his gran for me.

Penny Boden

My Fear Of Words

I had a computer given to me
It was an old one not new
So I started a computer corse
And they showed me what to do

Tyiping on my key broud
I was doing very well
Only did my name
That's all that I could spell

It is hard having a problem
People think you are thick
But I look for the little words
And that seems to do the trick

Frightning to fill a form in
That is me
But I manage to get around that
I say I carnt see

There are quiet a lot of people
That carnt read or spell
So don't be discoraged about it
You can still do well

So if you want to get on in life
This is what I do
I laugh about it to myslef
And that seems to get me threw

Knowning that there's help at hand
To take away those fears
On my own I managed this
Though it has taken me many years

So if you find you carnt read or spell
No, you might not be thick
It's more likely you have a condishon;
You are called, *'dislexic'*.

Barbara Jackson

The Morning Register

Miss Brown intoned the register
Like a softly murmured prayer.
Great trees in glades,
Curled ferns in shades,
And honest trades, were there.

On rocky plains with ancient names
Beneath jewelled skies we lay;
And the schoolhouse lane
Caressed by rain
Was as far as those stars away.

Tall and spare with greying hair
Miss Brown was kind but stern.
She gave me a priceless gift in the way
She made it a pleasure to learn.

In the morning light, her class was bright
With new images I could see.
Birds flew, fish swam, bold hammers rang,
And the register sang to me!

Tina Molli

Two Will One

Fingertips to tender skin,
tender skin to fingertips
touch, lips
converse
of forever.
Create a space.
Enrapture.
Discover, in togetherness,
mutual scenes unbounded
by time;
making time
apart,
eternity.

Tommy Frank O'Connor

Solitude Is A Welcome Caller

When your day has been just too much
And all you want to do is cry
The hours are going much too fast
Will I ever catch up?

Everyone is having a bad day
Tempers are frayed, clashes inevitable
We all wish the day would go away
Then there's a lull when you can stop and think

That's when I welcome solitude
Just to be you, sit and drift
Be able to forget things around you
Then solitude is a welcome caller.

Sit in your favourite retreat
Just let the day drift away
Smile, it's just you and the world
Nature welcomes you to sit and recoup.

How can you not be calm in the stillness?
No more worries, life is there for the living
Sit back, let the silence surround you
Close your eyes as you drift into peace

Then solitude is a welcome caller.

Carole A Cleverdon

2,000

I hope the world don't get worse
But besides intervention it will.
The sky is so beautiful
With clouds like mountains -
Serenity is there, it has to be
the sky tells me this:
Somewhere in the world
is beauty and purpose
And kind, gentle food
for the soul, the spirit
there are hearts bounded in
human kindness -
elation, joy, security
and peace.
Somewhere, sometime
I will find it.

Paul Barron

Life

Life begins as a little egg, no one knows what we will become or where we will be.
There is one thing that I do know and that is, if I were able to see what sort of world it was going to be, I would never have brought my kids in, to see drugs on every corner, murder in our street, war in all the countries, it's not even safe to sleep, always looking over your shoulder, never knowing who you will meet, wondering if the world is nice and neat, never knowing if the people you think you know are really how they seem, because deep down we really don't know the people we meet, we don't know if they're a drug dealer, murderer, rapist or pervert, even the people we love are never what they seem, so why is life so mean? Marriages everywhere are coming to an end, kids being torn apart in every corner of the world, some in homes, some on streets and most of the world is sharing poverty everywhere. Is that the sort of world that we want to meet?
Is it true what people say? Are we here to be tested in any way?
Is that why life is so cruel? Do we live in Hell? If so, I can't wait to go to Heaven where there is love peace and harmony.

Tina Harrison

THE VALLEY

Down in the valley of the several hundred days.
By the water meadow,
And the geese and swans that gaze,
And the snow upon the mountain,
And the autumn bonfire blaze.
Oh aye, we are singing for summer.

Peter Alfred Buss

The Butterfly

I watch as the butterfly emerges from her slumber
The life before she can no longer remember
Unfurling her wings in the midday sun
For the butterfly, her journey has just begun

As she flutters her wings, I smile and think that it won't be long
A gentle breeze and she will be gone
With each tentative beat of her wings, her new life calls
The leaf no longer an island, to the beauty in store

A breath of wind, the time is right
As I watch her winged dance out of sight
Life is so much more than what we perceive
We, too, are like the butterfly
If only we would believe

Nigel Basher

REFLECTION

Myriad hues of blazing sunset shining on the lake,
It shimmers o'er the waters.
A lonely tree,
A line.
It's only me,
The swimmers are my daughters,
Mirrored through amazing sunset signing off the day.

Hil Jennings

Tears Of Love

When it rains from Heaven above,
every drop's a drop of love,
a part of someone's heart and soul
that might have died years ago.
These drops of love are sent to us,
they fall upon our hearts,
so softly and gently, our hearts begin to swell.
That cup of love from Heaven above,
slowly filters through your veins.
As drops of love fall to the Earth
and land upon the ground,
you feel that nice sensation
that love is all around.

Robin Morgan

In Dreams

I see you when I least expect it
The sparks between us fly
There's no one around
To see our closeness
We walk together
You make me blush
You make me laugh
But most important, you make me smile
I don't want it to end
But I know when I awake
You won't be there
Togetherness only happens in my dreams
When I see you with your friends
And I am with mine
Our eyes meet
And my dreams become reality.

Sharon Atkinson

CHANGE OF HEAT

My body burned as love with me glowed,
Energising me to charm the heart from you,
But a shiver shook me as I nearer came,
It was cold to my touch, encased in an igloo.

My flaming fingertips no imprint made
Upon the icy oblivion of your eyes.
In frozen pools of blue no cracks appeared,
Your face just clouded over with my sighs.

Out on an iceberg, like a lone Pole star,
Your rigid, never-bending glare X-rayed
My white, consumed, evaporating frame
Which lost its heat as heat no power made.

The furnace in my heart was growing damp,
Shot icicles rained down to make it die,
An Arctic breeze blew change into my eyes,
But hope dies hard, one final surge I'd try

And so I came, with love's rekindled embers,
Prepared to chisel through your frosted glass.
But the ground was green, your frozen fort had melted,
And you had gone, no more this way to pass.

And I, a snow queen now, immobile, numb,
Stand rooted, starving, here while you and she
Migrate on summer's wings to warmer climes.
She thawed you out. I froze in sympathy.

Barbara White

A WALK UP THE HILL

It's not a big hill, by any standards
But when you're three and a half years old
It can be a pretty daunting prospect.
As you slowly climb to the top, his small hand
Resting safely in yours,
The questions begin.
'What's that Grandad?'
Rings out time and again.
What you don't know
You *carefully* make up
Because you know he'll remember your answer.

At the top
The questions become statements
Look at: the cows, the sheep, the horses
The farms dotted on the hillside
The village station
His other grandparents' farm across the valley.
This hilltop panorama
Hold no beauty for him, no magic.
It's just there; it's where he lives, his natural surroundings.
Its majesty may, one day, hit his senses, but for now it's just
'Can we go for a walk up the hill, Grandad?'

Alan McKean

MEMORIES

He knows no more pain
He knows no more sorrow.
I'm glad I was with him,
There is no tomorrow.

Rarely alone, but able to hear,
It was an honour to nurse him
And defuse his fear.

His wife will be fretting
Missing her man.
But she has her memories
Of adorable Stan.

No one can take them,
They are locked in her heart,
'Twas a sad day indeed
When they had to part.

Janice Melmoth

Missing Love

Thousand times to be apart,
Thousand times to cry,
I feel so deserted,
Cos you are far away,
And I can't hold you tight.
But nothing can take you out,
Of my mind and heart.
O' Dear! Send me a thousand kisses,
You are my veins,
You are my lifeline,
Never say goodbye, Dear.
Come with me,
Come, let's build the world of our dreams
For you and me.
Let's enjoy the fragrance of the blooming flowers,
And let's take care of our years,
Dear, tomorrow will surely be ours.

Vanlalfaka Arakan

JOURNEY

Looking upon you I find a light of mine,
Desperation creeps in and fragility is open.
Thoughts of happiness trying for air, precious.
Can't see trees, green blinds me on a summer's day,
Lying in wait for the waiting, peace of mind ready to leave for a song,
Wanting life is feeling whole, paints an image of tiny hope.
Loving lightness, heavy rain,
Trying, fighting, meeting pain.
Light breeze faintly waiting, time to force the hour of dark.
Nightmares creep into consciousness, forcing breaking light,
Eyes of glass crying in the night.
Making waves of golden shore, deeper than the depths of ever,
Brightness finds me hiding, waiting, wanting end of sight and time,
Finding ways to fill the whiteness, glaring brightness over me.
I yearn to leave in sweeping journey, running to the turning free,
And witness in my own understanding a lightness deep inside of me.
My hands, deep valleys, my eyes are caves,
Though empty I refuse to be.
The air is thick, the breathing hard, choking, fighting, hollow, deep,
I try to push back; thoughts are waning, in fighting life embraces me.
Closing down, the whiteness fading, colour fills the fog of old,
I cannot write, my words fail me,
Yet lines of endless weaving beauty circle deep inside of me.
Inside is safe, shimmering, glowing,
How do I put an end to greys?
Sea of souls in endless waking, faking but I always see,
I hear the soft melody, smiling sadly, and yet the light, if slight, I see.

Lesley Ebbage

SOLVING MYSELF

An empty feeling has settled in my stomach, refusing to let go. A feeling that never becomes satiated, feeding on my insecurity, growing every minute. I scream in desperation, in frustration, at the hopelessness that has caught me in a grip, impossible to to handle. Longing for a culmination that will mean an end to my inexplicable depression.

Sometimes I wonder whether it ever gets easier, even though I know I have been here before. Should I not be able to cope by now? But is that the point? At times it feels as if I long for these empty feelings because, in a sense, I know them, I can handle them. In a twisted sort of way they symbolise one of the few things I can grasp in life. Besides the lust for love.

Is it not strange how we cling on to the few certain things in life, even though they might be detrimental? How I wish I could dissect the unconscious mind, to find some answers to the questions that elude me.

Why is that one of the hardest things in life is actually understanding yourself? Coming to terms with whom and what you are. Knowing thyself should surely be the easiest thing, given how confusing the world already is. I am truly a bewildered soul.

Now and again my inner self plays tricks on me. Making me feel as if I can almost grasp the reasoning behind my own actions. But somehow it always slips away, leaving me more confused than ever before. If only I could always see the world as clearly and free of trouble as when I have the arms of my love around me. Enveloping me in a cloak of security I have found nowhere else.

Filip Aggestam

2

seems to me that for a while there
time forgot us, didn't it?
left us to idle in the waters,
wrapped up in the warmth of the air
outside the world almost, and left knowing always
knowing, that i wanted to be no other place but there
with you
those velvet days in each other's circle, like a venn diagram
like something out of an old poem
i think, really, i've never been so happy
but time did catch us up, didn't it?
as we knew, as we knew -
the brightest flowers don't live so long,
better, i suppose, to be the green leaf
to weather, to maintain
not that i believe that at all.

Lee Rodgers

Faith

Bruises fade although the pain still remains.
I still remember every time you'd hit me with that long wooden cane.
Thrown against cold stairs, it constantly felt like I was on an
electric chair.

Every day I was afraid to wake up and leave what I thought was my
only source of comfort, the only place I felt safe.
I would sit there bottled up with the only hope for me in the world,
the little thing called 'faith'.

I would dream of happy days, free from abuse
Wondering if there was going to be a day only full of truce . . .

It's that time of day again, it's just turned 10 o'clock
My father is going to walk in from work, which is the local pub
on the other side of the dock.
'Where is she, the little wretch? I'm gonna get you,' he cries.
I'm sitting up here, shaking, hoping I will die.

He comes upstairs, throws me a few fists.
Look at how he turns just after a few drinks!

It's too late now, I'm lying on the floor
I've been beaten up again, but this time it's much worse than before.
There's nothing left here for me, the thought suddenly fills my head,
Maybe it's God's way of telling me I soon shall be dead?

'That was the last round,' I whisper, 'my faith has all run out.'
As I lie on the floor wriggling and squiggling about.
The last thing I think about is the ticking of the clocks
Then my eyes slowly close and my heart finally stops.

Bianca Pymont

Sanity Redeem

Look upon gold as man's foolish dream,
succumb to the greed of the rich not me,
don't shun me cos I have nowt and you have plenty,
for I know love and comfort of life,
and I know where this will take thee,
open your eyes to the card called 'credit'
follow like sheep in a line for debt, baa,
charity at home is where it begins,
do not line the pockets of the aristocracy,
their coats, they are heavy from weight of their own wealth,
made upon the public called Joe,
and where is Jane Doe in all this, she is down, chin on floor,
fetch the broom, sweep upon her brow, lift her spirit,
let the next swipe, swipe it clean,
this thing called 'credit' not points, but sanity redeem.

Janette Fisher

The Orchard

Fleshy, full-bodied fruit adorns branches
as a game bird, ripe for plucking.
Its garish colours, like a foppish dandy,
as it basks in the reflected glory
of the sun's lustrous rays.

Within this tree-lined labyrinth,
I watched, transfixed, beguiled
by a vision of your sylph-like form
in a diaphanous dress, an ethereal
presence amongst lofty branches.

The sky, cloudless cerulean,
and I, so insignificant, against
this bountiful backdrop of beauty,
trees harbouring their harvest,
bestowing gifts on the unworthy.

Engulfed by the vast expanse,
my mind cascading thoughts
like Niagara Falls, mirrors
the dropping of fruit to earth,
waking me from my reverie.

Paul Burton

Hands Across The Ocean

Hands across the ocean, hearts across the sea.
Though we've never met, you mean the world to me.

It's only been nine months, since you first e-mailed me,
But we have been so close and strong, like it was meant to be.

We may not be real sisters, but believe you me,
We can trace our family tree, back to Mother Eve.

Some people say we look alike, while others disagree,
We have so much in common, what with calligraphy.

I think of you each passing day, across the deep blue sea,
I wonder what you think of me, or is that vanity?

With each e-mail and phone call, we save our sanity,
Oh, sister dear, I really wish, that you lived closer to me!

Angie Lambert

Something Or Nothing

Appearances of death can be proved false,
Defibrillators can restore a pulse,
The leafless tree revives itself in spring,
With each new dawn the birds awake and sing.

Conductorless, an orchestra will find
It takes a while to get themselves in time,
So it's too early to admit defeat,
Before our hearts have synchronised their beat.

A newborn baby often shuts its eyes,
But there's no hurt where there is no surprise,
As flowers always take some time to bloom,
But nothing grows, if it's not given room.

Elastic bands will stretch before they snap
And we recycle now before we scrap.
As magnets can attract of can repel,
To fall out means you liked me once as well.

The door is closed but only on the latch,
The perfect throw awaits the perfect catch.
Like two ships sailing on a different tack,
But not too late for you to call me back.

Chris Scriven

The School Bell

Standing with the bunch of mums
Smokers, chatterers and you,
All dutifully awaiting the excited din
Of another school day through.
Different to you,
Same squashed-up voices as children sing,
Wet smudgy artwork in stubby fingers,
Coats as capes of superheroes and PE bags swing.

This afternoon you met that man again.
Stole precious hours with your lover.
Upon on this usual feint hopscotched playground
You got here in a whirl only to discover
That everyone stares at you like they know.
How can they? Beyond anything they would ever guess.
They only get to shop and clean between school bells.
See now how his kisses accentuate your breasts.

You try to remember his look as you left
Him exactly, lazy-limbed on a stained bed,
Eyes staring at the swirling patterned floor
All the things that are left unsaid.
How he hates to see you dress.
You rummaging for your keys.
Then you step outside and feel exposed
In the awkward eyes of these strangers.

Wildly look for him in your rear view mirror
As you drive fast away, like from a crime.
You want to see him running after you,
But he never does. You just looking for a sign.
But he has a wife, things he can't leave
Not even for you and you should never have asked.
You remember how you nodded in understanding
Through the tears you had fought so hard to mask.

And now you stand and wait for your children
Clutch them harder, suggesting sweets on the way home.
Driving you smile as you squeeze their day from them
And all through it you glance desperately at your phone.
You want him to ring to say he cares,
To say how he misses the curve of your back.
You can smell his hands in your hair,
His tongue still ringing in your ear.

C S Rowland

By The Sea

(For Mum)

Blessed,
Holy way of gentleness
Here, where sea
Gathers into calmness.

Gulls circle like
Searching questions - call
Eyes to edge of surging
Expanse vast-like

Mind moving slowly
To comfort of truth light
Where heart of creation
Can move in moment near the sea.

George Coombs

How Hard It Is To Talk To You

To feel so sensitive that the sun does not even burn,
the hot water does not scold,
the ice, one hair does not raise . . .

But.

To feel so sensitive that every word you vomit out,
becomes some disgusting remnant.
A pile left behind.
A rank and loathing
mess
of expression and misunderstanding.
An unexplained stench on the floor,
that people turn their forgiveness up at.

I fetched my dustpan and brush
I
tried to sweep up the mess.
Wished I could cook the sick and eat my words.
Munch them back into my being.
Or somehow,
fetch a sick bag
and catch the words down my shirt.

Instead however,
I sneezed
and
the words,
dribbled down your chin.

Anna Bosworth

ANOREXIA

Sickness rises inside of me.
Rejection in your eyes.
Turn away and carry on.
I cannot eat today.
My stomach churns with hunger,
My thoughts drift to your betrayal.
I suppress the need to eat,
The need to live.
I feel it grow inside of me.
Alone and left to bear.
A gentle soul has turned cold,
I cannot eat today -
I try to smile and laugh through the pain,
My laughter cannot last.
I think of you walking away.
I cannot eat today -
I shut my eyes and see your intimacy,
A knife twists in my womb.
Left alone tonight,
I cannot eat today -
And so the time that passes,
Leaves me weak for you,
I start to float away.
I cannot eat today -
A rejection so deep.
It cuts my very life from me,
A pain so strong
I cannot eat.

Elly Fenton

ETERNITY

It has been an eternity
Since I saw her smile
An eternity since I said goodbye.

It has been an eternity
Since my tears began to flow
An eternity since I let her go.

All I really desired was to see her grow
Away from disease, starvation, the infected fly
Oh why should children have to die?

In my heart I knew it was time
        To give up the fight
My prayer is they tell her of her birthright.

Although she has travelled a thousand miles
I carry a vivid picture of her innocent smile.
Forever I will not forget my precious one.
I know the pain will remain
For I will not see my daughter again

This is *my* eternity.

Elaine Priscilla Kilshaw

WHAT IS LIFE?

Life is too short to live it without fun.
Life is too nice to fill it with deep sorrow.
Life is too colourful not to try to notice it.
Life is too serious not to take any advice from somebody.
Life is a boat by which man goes to the great ocean
full of ups and downs.

Vineta Priedíte

Do You Remember?

Mum - do you remember - when I was just a girl
How you would stand for hours and hours - just brushing at my curls?

Mum - do you remember - putting rollers in each tress
And when they all got tangled up, no curls, just frizzy mess?

Mum - do you remember - when you walked me to school
I would always cry and scream, you must have felt a fool?

Mum - do you remember, each year our holidays
Were spent at Denes in Kessingland - we'd sleep in our chalet?
On talent night, you'd always sing, we all loved your strong voice
The audience would clap and cheer, clearly their first choice.

Mum - do you remember - when my babies came along
Always being there for me - on days when things went wrong?

Mum - do you remember - always being there on hand?
That's why you were so special, the best mum in the land.

Dad - do you remember - when I'd sit upon your knee?
I'd snuggle up so close to you, while you read books to me.

Dad - do you remember - the allotment you worked on?
You took me down to help you - I got chased by that white swan

Dad - do you remember - when I passed my driving test?
I paid half for my first car - you helped me pay the rest

Dad - do you remember - when you'd pick me up each day?
I'd just had my first baby - at your house I would stay

Dad - do you remember - going walking with my children?
I hope you know they truly thought you were - a grandad in a million

Memories are all I have - they're with me constantly
That's why I pray with all my heart - you remember loving me.

Diane Crouch

Outsider

The world revolves while you stand and watch
You step in and it moves aside
It's not all bad to simply observe
You don't get caught in the ride

Outside can be a lonely place
Inside it looks so warm
Log fires don't burn forever though
They soon go out in a storm

For those not taken in by the crowd
For those on the outside looking in
Hold your head high
Let the world pass you by
Courage will allow you to win.

Emily Watts

Mad

She walks around,
Her eyes wandering.
Is she mad?
She stops,
And pauses,
Then walks on.
Is she mad?
The people she sees,
Laugh and point.
Is she mad?
She sits down,
And cries softly,
Is she mad?
The people see,
But don't stop,
Is she mad?
She picks herself up
But then drops down again,
Is she mad?
She walks into a room and sits down,
And is silent,
Is she mad?
She opens a book
And reads softly,
She is alone.

Louisa Thorne (12)

Whispering Breeze

Sweet whispering of an evening breeze,
Lightly caressing all that it sees,
Like invisible fingers, a touch of a feather,
Soothing, bringing mind and body together.

Leaves on the trees give it a voice,
Hushed, yet clear, what is said is your choice.
Grass and corn gently sway,
As it passes quietly on its way.

Across the land, picking up every sound.
Carries the voices of country and town,
This breeze, mystic in its charm,
In its wake, leaves a tranquil calm.

This gentle drifting of nature's air,
Ambling, meandering, all to share.
As in all of nature, it has its own way,
From early dawn, to the end of day.

It has no beginning or an end,
But just to drift and to blend.
From the warmth of summer, to winter freeze,
Is the calm, of a whispering breeze . . .

Alan J Morgan

THE EDGE

Primitive reality swept the land.
Bogus beauty in all human conceptuality
We know and yet we do not.
Regret the harvest of past actions
And beauty the edge of all beholding.
Gathered round the fire of human activity
Flames licking upward - reaching.
Searching for the impossible.
Nothing found but where we are.

Clive Cornwall

MIDNIGHT ANGER

Called out at well past three,
Ambulance, Fire and Police there be,
Neighbours moan to all those there,
As blue words colour the midnight air,
Everyone swears and stamps the ground,
Tempers flare, it knows no bound,
Policemen bang loudly on the door,
Ambulance men lay stretchers on the floor,
The Fire brigade fresh from their strike,
Run ladders out, 'what are they like?'
Then when they simply can't be heard,
They all yell loudly on the word,
But it's no good and give up in vain,
At the sound of their sleep's bane,
'It's no damned use,' they grimly say,
'Now we'll have to move away.'
For in the house there lives Nora,
Who is Yorkshire's loudest snorer.

Mel Price

Proper Bastards

Very good at hiding it
for several wily years
you saucy bedroom lepers

and still able to criticise others
for their antisocial behaviour while
you are busy cremating your vows

In the burning flames of lust.
You swapped your gold for brass
to lie with your bit on the side.

You also lie through the enamel
of your false laughing teeth when
you blow sweet kisses to your kids

when they leave the house for school.
They oblivious to your capers destroying
this precious institution and hopefully

they will learn the difference
between loyalty and deception;
unlike you. Proper bastards.

Francis Hughes

Diminuendo

Today the air itself aches like a groin
for the love that stripped away all pride.
Though you sleep with a half-dead thing you call your soul,
it seems the appetites live on -
lust that's rendered concentrate with age.
Meanwhile the chorus of reason gloats:
You should be grateful for what you had - it may
so easily have never been.
Sometimes the missing can be seen, almost:
a shock of spectral light that falls
between those intervals of birch that list
a dozen yards away in the autumn breeze.

Ian Harrow

DIRTY OLD BOOTS

I drove through the country on a sunny day,
Wild rabbits gambolled in fields of hay,
Admiring the trees and the bushes so dense
And a pair of old boots alone on a bench
How did they get there, I wonder and stare,
I look for the owner but nobody's there,
They're dirty, well-worn with laces tied neat
Has the person who left them now got sore feet?
I grind to a halt and I look all around,
Almost too frightened to utter a sound,
They look so deserted placed neatly just there
Not just the one, but a lovely old pair
I sit down beside them, curiosity abounds,
And all I can hear are the countrified sounds
A tiny field mouse scampers over my toes
Birds sing in the trees and a wasp's on my nose
I flick it away and with hand to my brow
I glance at the boots sat beside right now
Time's not on my side, I'm running so late
I'll be back tomorrow and that's a date
But, when I return there's no sign of them there
Did somebody find them? Did somebody care?
I search all around me with eyes like a hawk
But those dirty old boots must have gone for a walk.

Jackie Davies

Operation Christmas Child

The children of Eastern Europe
Had a volunteer in place,
As they opened their shoeboxes
Delight spread over their face.

One little boy from Russia
Just sat with his shoebox,
Then slowly tried to open it
As if undoing locks.

Once inside, he found a car
And a trailer too,
He played with the Rolo
As he didn't know what to do.

He shuffled closer and closer
To the willing volunteer
And put his head on his shoulder,
He really was that near.

For a few brief moments
The man gave the boy his love,
Perhaps something he'd never known
From parents in Heaven above.

He hadn't said a single word
And then they found out
That the boy couldn't talk,
Of that there was no doubt.

He is just a single child
Helped by one shoebox,
Multiply it by thousands
And see the value of the stocks!

Rita Hardiman

Traffic Jam

Stuck in a traffic jam, barely moving at all,
if we do, it's only a crawl.
We want to get home, we've had a long day,
visiting relatives nearly two hundred miles away.

Perhaps we should have stayed, but we like to do it in a day,
however, we cannot control the obstacles thrown in our way,
the inevitable, but unexpected, traffic delay.

The weather plays its part,
one minute it is light, the next it is dark,
lights on then lights off, it's like a game we play,
oh, how we long to end this day.

Tired, exhausted, tempers fray,
hopefully we'll be home soon,
thankfully tomorrow is another day.

Julie Marie Laura Shearing

The Weary Way

the word is in a cycle
within stand men
and animals and nature
without its space
and an endless time

but if the world is in a cycle
endless and nothing can strike it
from its course
then men may falter and die
the earth moves on regardless

so if we're to progress
on this earth
we must endeavour to
leave our earthly boundary
in some sense

be it spiritual or scientific means
man will one day leave
this world's confines
and enter into space
and an endless time.

D Finlay

SPACES

Emptiness stares,
From that far wall,
Like wilderness,
A window would add dimension,
Help heal the nothingness.

The space that glares,
From off that wall,
Grips quietly,
As all thought seems in suspension,
With no safe place to hide.

A painting there,
Upon that space,
Could well inspire,
Bold adventurous intention,
Changing the mood and pace.

To sands or seas,
Or lands unknown,
Real or imagined extension,
To visit when I please.

Kathleen M Scatchard

'Come Over Here, Boy! The Battle Has Begun' Said The Patriotic Racist, To His Idolising Son

You'll live by tribal standards, tribal doctrine, tribal law
And thus from influence external, you'll defend your tribal shore
When forced you unto corner, shall you wage your tribal war
For you're the nature of the tribe, and nothing more!

You'll disregard of others, if their ways, they'll not desert
For though you preach and teach for hours
Unto yours, they'll not convert
Much better are they, that abide in a way
That believe they will keep them from hurt
Than them that would kneel, on the ground at your feet
And embrace, but your sacred . . . dirt!

The more adhered unto commune, be it country, church or team
The more adverse you'll be to others, be without
You'll revel in your triumphs, as you chase your perfect dream
And unto those that be without, you'll rest your doubt!

Upon pedestals, pulpits and terraces
Stand the angry, complacent and proud!
Taunting their victims to feed on the seed
Of the crop from the field they have ploughed.
So certain are they, in their way, that they play
That they voice unto others, out loud!
Leading poor sheep into darkness and sleep
When but all did they seek . . . was a crowd!

Be you patriotic, be you racist in your heart!
I pray that others, on your turf, shall never tread
Obsessive and erratic, will you tear their limbs apart
Or simply, kick them in their heads, until they're dead.

So proud of your nation, religion, your team
Will rejoice you, each conquest, you win
But many have died, whilst of glory, they cried
Never knowing that . . . *pride* . . . is a sin!

Mark Anthony Noble

THE POWER OF PEACE

The power of peace should never cease,
Sounds of trumpets will not fade.
I hear people's voices shout out loud and clear,
We will not fear the power of peace, it will be with us today,
And ever more, the power of peace is strong, so many voices
can't be wrong.
With banners held high we reach the sky.
Onward marches happy throng filled with happy songs.
And we knew we could go on, and we had to wave those flags.
We would shout and we would sing, to our beliefs we would
surely cling.
It must be our right to fight for our plight.
Tomorrow we will just keep moving on.
Sleepers awake, there is no time to quiver and shake, the wind of
change
is blowing
Right.
Don't listen to those dark condemning voices you hear.
Sing the words that you know are right, they only wait for you to set
them free.
The power of peace should never cease.

B Ashford

HOLLY

Holly wasn't well today, she was in a lot of pain,
Her mother bought her medicine to make her well again.
She took a spoonful of the stuff, all dark and rich and thick,
But the nasty stuff played up her tum and made her blooming sick.
So, Holly, just get better soon, that's what we all do say,
And if you're feeling well enough, you can go out to play.

Mick Gayfer

The Modern Workplace

(Welcome to the revolution!)

At my interview Mr Manager boldly strutted around stating,
'We are only here like team players.
We don't want generals, leaders, artists, thinkers, poets, or even mythical dragon slayers.
What we need are sheep, furry and white, who will bleat and always follow this company code.
Why, some of our senior execs still call for Mummy and burst out crying when crossing the road.

Remember, there is no I in team my dear young man, you must only think in our own trusted way.
Sit in your pen from 9 to 5. If you have an opinion, keep quiet, we don't want to hear your say.
Some of us have been here for well over a century still working on perfecting that profit and loss.
Why, Jenkins, there is well over two hundred, every morning we have to scrape off the fresh moss.

And so where do you see yourself, young man, when Halley's Comet is to make its next show?
Do you want a lifetime of knowledge, experience and travel? All together now scream, *'No!'*
You want to join with us, and every day see a bit more of the life drained from your own soul.
Here are the dice of your life, my son, don't dream, don't think, don't give them a role.

All our managers here never say a thing, they just cc the boss on every day's exciting caper.
Just today, I had an email from one, telling me he had ordered some more of the lined paper.

So put it there, young man, and join the walking dead of this and
every modern-day British firm.
For don't you know that you are now in a prison, and you, young man,
have been given a life-term.'

Andrew Manzi

SANCTUARY

Amidst the mantle of the clouds I found my heaven.
Enshrouded by the fog as it became my shawl,
My blanket. Security.
Sandwiched amongst the delicate softness that held the ferocity
of Leveret
But had the potential to become a lion, brutal and powerful,
It chose to protect me.
A sanctuary, from where the only way was down,
Not Mother Earth herself could tear me from this Eden.
High above the serpents and the wolves, I needed no god to
Protect me.
Joey in the pouch could not be safer than I.
I had the world at my feet, I saw eternity and it astounded me.
The beauty of the world seeped through everything misshapen
and monstrous.
It rose to meet me as the mist that leaves the canopy to join the stars.
It brought home to my heart and I'll never be lonely again.
Ended is my quest for someone or thing that will
Protect me.
It was there. It is here.

Rhian Watkins

VOLCANO

The ground shakes,
The mountain breaks,
As hot ash forces its way down,
Towards the burning ground.

A long pile of rock temporarily stops
The burning flames,
From spreading around.

The only hope of safety is the river of ice,
That borders the once busy city.

Now the river of ice,
That holds the heat at bay melts,
As people run towards the sea,
As their forest of buildings of glass,
Sinks below the hot burning ash.

Andrew James Ball

A Message From Beyond The Gravé

Hate
late
plate
fate
chocolate
crate
slate
ate
congregate
rate
and
even
mate
but
not
paté.

Jonathan Harper

THE WORLDLY END

Now the body is withered, the hair is grey;
But the mind is very much alert.
I am no longer young, I know,
But my conscience is still awfully hurt!
The average span of human life, they say,
Is seventy years or so.
I have exceeded my fare, I know,
But where did the duration go?
I don't seem to have tarried so long,
And the past appears a vague dream.
Eternal life is sure to follow, I know,
And that time span is somewhat extreme!
Deep within me, my soul is content,
I don't fear the Angel of Death.
He is sure to come, I know,
But he is welcome to take my breath!
I have believed and worked the best deeds,
Praise be to God who has mercifully guided.
Had I been one of the rebellious, I know,
The Fire of Hell is for the deluded!

Umar Azam

My Greek Island

I'm at the airport and I'm delighted
My treasured Greek island and I are to be reunited
Year after year I must return
It tugs and pulls and makes me yearn
The smell in the air of herbs and spices
A bus ride to the boat, then we're afloat
It's dark in the night and I am on deck
As we travel on, daylight breaks through
What a sight to see, light dancing on the water
It's calm and still
Many times I've done this but it still gives me a thrill
We arrive at the harbour, there taxis are waiting
To take me on a short ride
I hear the tinkle of bells as goats amble by
Around a few bends and we're on top of the hill
Looking down on Kalymnos so pretty and still
The sight is still awesome; I'm holding my breath
I didn't realise, now I know I've finally arrived
The people are so friendly and helpful to all
Both cheeks kissed and arms opened wide
The welcome they give you is second to none
So many friends arrive that I've met over the years
To be together with our Greeks
It's the people who draw us back year after year
And I'm delighted
My treasured Greek island and I are reunited.

Carol Hanney

A Childhood Myth?

I looked for it in relatives,
And also in my friends,
Results were always negative,
My searching had no end,
Its absence causes great distress,
Throughout the world each day,
Destroying people's happiness,
And bringing great dismay,
It's banished from my mind forthwith,
It simply cannot stay,
It's nothing but a childhood myth,
This thing they call 'fair play'!

Matthew L Burns

HANBURY WOODS

Many people talk of this wood
Is it me or have we misunderstood
From deep in the trees
To the birds and the bees
Maybe it's a place where we just have fun!
Although there is a myth and a legend about this place
It's dirty old Reg flashing without a trace
Twelve till one
After the witching hour's gone
Is it me?
Because it's still this creepy old place.

Mark Roberson

NITRAM

Silence speaks a lot
I know you really care
It's like you have a knot
That you can't really bear

I wish you could talk
Show me how you really feel
One day I might walk
And the pain may heal.

Zoe Laing

Perfect Moment

Our bodies merge as one together,
I long to stay this way forever.
You'll hold me tight and keep me safe,
Throughout bad times and stormy weather.

Outside the window pours heavy rain,
Without you it's always the same.
But when you're here and pressed against me,
I shed no tears and feel no pain.

Longing to feel your amazing kiss.
My mouth gently meets your perfect lips,
A kiss so soft yet passionate.
Will I ever again feel a moment as beautiful as this?

Lee Byway

Rooked

Take what with you as you will
Whereas what mine you take it still
Gone so far your hidden lair
My powers cease to find me there

And on this night I lie aware
And think of how stripped was I bare
Though tender thoughts I take to hand
Never be enough for this man damned

Life slipped through fingers did - like sand
Shattered the heart like glass - was planned
The love shone bright as white finish - look
It was mine to give where you just took

Am I not a monarch of this life, mistook
Position shifted, a castled rook
A fallen chipping of a sculpture filed
Which shapes your life, my life, or child?

Gary Crossan

On The Road To Fifteen

Only fourteen and nowhere to go
only a child with needs
how many like this I ponder and learn
in dismay reality hits?

Only fourteen and abandoned
to what or whom, who's to say?
A cruel world awaits, if we hesitate
there may not be one more day.

Only fourteen, how could this be?
Mere blood and bone for the heap
within this child a world of dreams
so much to offer and reap.

Only fourteen, can I think that far back?
Comfort, food, TV and love
remembered, cherished, amazed and impressed
at a world so willing to give.

Only fourteen, no decisions to make
peanut butter, jam or milk
after school fun and holiday sun
and the magic of all its ilk.

Only fourteen, a courtroom of people
arguing and deciding what's best
does anyone care? Does anyone spare
a thought for this child's quest?

Only fourteen, love needed and given
a guiding hand, simple and pure
how much does it take to relieve the heartache
to make this child feel assured.

Only fourteen.

Stevan Leonard Payne

Mask On The Wall

A mask on the wall
Hides a once beautiful race forgotten
A sad one with limbs like cotton.
The haunted eyes say, ‘Give us food!’
The hungry cry, ‘Give us water, we are dry.’
The scorched earth can no longer produce corn
The mother has no milk for her newborn
Bellies swollen, limbs like sticks
Stagnant water full of disease
Broken bodies, broken souls
Hearts are aching for one’s child
The child that won’t see morning
The mother, the father, the son
Dead and gone forever
Because no one cared enough!
All that is left of this proud race is
A mask on the wall.

Pat Seddon

WHISPERS OF LIGHT

Walking under God's sky
Man's feet on life's soil
Eroding pathways stretch for miles
Animals rear up, butterflies flutter
Daffodils yellow and vibrant
Bees buzzing, dancing lively about
Colours, green, brown, across the hills
Wild hawthorn's suffocating sweet scent
Redwings greedily eating
Unstoppable trees pushing through
Pounding rain comes with force
Camouflaged viaducts lie disused
Boggy moors hold times past and present
Castles still stand proud
Stone walls complete the scenery
Ripe blackberries ready for picking
Shadows cast from the evening light
Reflecting coastline widespread and vast
Stirred silence, mild as a prayer
On this land we tread.

Sharron Hollingsworth

One Gifted Day

The quiet of dawn is broken, on a fine winter's morn,
As we chance to look at daylight, with a timely tired yawn,
A nose outside the bedclothes, soon time to getting out,
With a tempting ray of sunshine, to help us move about.

A glance behind the curtain, a feeling of do or die,
Outside in the coldness, above, a bright blue sky,
Mist in soft profusion, still lies in hollows white,
It lightens as it drifts off, with the passing of the night.

The sight is just as angels, with flowing fleecy gowns,
The stillness of the morning, no wind to make a sound,
Golden edges forming, on Stirling range of hills,
As the sun makes first approaches, to cheer the morning still.

Breakfast soon is over, now work is on our minds,
With a smile, and feeling happy, being healthy, 'sublime'
Having a job to go to, there is nothing to compare,
Beats standing in a dole queue, for handouts, I would not dare!

Hard day's work is over, good earnings without shame!
Feeling a wee bit piddly, got soaked in pouring rain,
Travelling home all soggy, soaked right to the skin,
Hope coughs and sneezes stay away, drying off, I had to grin.

Again we check the blankets, shower for the night,
Once more glance behind the curtains, checking all is right,
Evening mist now creeping night lights look severe.
Soon the sounds of night are echoing, down one visible ear.

Alex Wilson

LATENT TREACHERY

Beware the latent treachery
of those you call your own
and keep on smiling when they destroy
the friendship you have shown.

Peter Royston Cole

Throwing Stones

Lines on the paper,
Point to my new low,
Of hopes dashed by silence,
Where once stood your noise.
Lower my accord,
For I hate your ways,
Wicked witch of there,
In my loving dreams.
Conscious commitment to your despise,
Banging on your soulless walls,
In hope, despair and hatred.
I love you.
Sunstroke and superior,
Not yet gone,
And not yet beyond your grasp.
I love you.

Matthew Richards

BEAUTIFUL SIN

The fiercest threat to mankind,
Are beautiful sins that grind?
Of the sins we see and condemn
As architects, our own faults are found in them.
Look at the sick souls in castle,
You'll see what bustled, useless to haggle.
It is good to see friends float in pride,
But greater pain to see them lose their stride.
What is beautiful is not salacious,
Beware! What is sin can be fallacious,
Like tales from a street sister's seductive lips,
That gives hearts sobs from wrong tips.
Beware! It is beautiful sin to seek security,
That cannot guarantee eternity . . .

A beautiful sin is not only cracked by liars,
That makes God sceptical of His name-bearers.
A beautiful sin isn't those case awaiting trials,
After eternal silence of the victims of betrayals.
While the engineers brag with gain less gains,
I see the world of victims groove in pains.
A beautiful sin is not only fibs that killed sanity,
But anything that slays the heart of unity.
Avoid them, 'cause they are vastly, canny,
And unusually funny.
It destroys law and ingenuity,
To achieve cheap popularity.
Yes! Sin is anything rotten,
That looks seemingly golden . . .

It is lust to love and desire,
What we cannot tolerate and acquire.
To save a dying soul is so beautiful,
But to keep a page of the debt is awful
When we can give what from others,
We crave to acquire without bothers.

It is a sin to accuse the earth's decay,
To be the wicked will of God bitter delay.
It is sin to feel arrived here without fears,
Where A-Day-Born abhors with tears.
If you must love, give all,
And like Christ, take a sacrificial fall.

Anyatonwu Ikechukwu Collins

At What Age?

What is it that leads us to places ungone,
And helps us to turn in decisions so wrong,
Guides to blame others when inside we know,
The blame is on us and our faces must show?

What is it that forces us chances to take,
To soil one bed as another we make,
To risk precious life on prizes minute,
As again and again in our foot we shoot?

What is it that tells us to challenge a dare,
To walk full into fire not showing scare,
To win at all cost without asking reason,
A time in the light of some passing season?

What is it that finally does settle us down
Cause response with accompanying frown,
Bring home the danger of the vast adventures,
Arrival of kids or the glass filled with dentures?

Denise K Mitchell

One Year Old

One year old
This little man
Mischief! Mischief!
Is his name.
Cupboards and tables are bare
Nothing is safe from this little man
He clears the decks
Not a cupboard door safe
From his enquiring eyes
Saucepans are scattered
All over the place
Nothing is safe from this little man
With that cheeky grin
That lights up his face
With that innocent look,
What have I done?
As he chatters away
In a language all his own
A bundle of energy from dawn to dusk
This adorable little man
One year old today

P D Turner

Spider

Now, I guess you think a spider,
Is not a lot of fun.
But to some spider mother,
He's her darling little one.
So, do not step upon him,
Or poke him in fun,
Remember, to his mother
He's her precious tiny one.

And if he's skidding in your bath
With terror in his soul,
Please don't turn the tap on,
And flush him down the hole,
Then walk away really happy
Content with what you've done.
Remember you're just drowning,
Some fragile mother's son.

Understand a spider,
Is not a small boys' pet,
In his world he's important
And to him you're just a threat
So, do not step upon him
Or poke at him in fun.
Remember, to his mother
He's her darling spider son.

Mary Buckley-Clarke

A Good Movie

There's nothing like a good movie,
With a good girlfriend,
Or a good wife,
If you 'ave one,

Even if watching alone,
A good movie,
Will make a strong impression,
On your mind

You'll be transformed,
In other words, 'feel a kick'.
In about an hour
In a fantasy world,
Of make-believe

A good movie,
With a good story
Makes you want to live,
Par excellence!

An superb movie,
Makes a good story,
Come alive,
It'll make you want,
To believe in it,
With all your heart

You just can't wait,
Or beat,
A good movie,
You can only
Just get a kick out of it.

John Floyd

THE BEAUTIFUL AND WONDERFUL TAJ MAHAL!

Ardently and madly in love with his wife, Mumtaz Mahal,
Shajahan wanted her to remain by his side always,
Believing that her presence had inspired and motivated him,
To shoulder upon his heavy responsibilities as Emperor!

He considered her to be his prized possession,
To own up and to shower honours upon her,
To adore and admire her loudly and proudly,
In recognition and appreciation of his adoration and admiration towards her!

He was never ever mentally prepared,
To even envisage the thought,
Of her succumbing to the pressure tactics of death,
Leaving aside the likelihood of her pre-deceasing him!

As the mysterious Goddess of Death had a peculiar style,
To catch and snatch away the life of anybody,
Her unexpected operation to separate her from him,
Was really an unbearable body blow to him!

Stunned and shocked at her loss,
He was not at all ready to accept,
The factual positional painful reality,
That she was not in his midst anymore!

To give her rebirth and resurrection,
To flog and flag off his spirits,
Which he had lost on her passing away,
He constructed the beautiful and wonderful Taj Mahal!

Davis Akkara

UNTITLED

Not everyone who wanders is lost,
Not all those who are dead are forgot.
You know, all that glitters - not necessarily gold
And the greatest stories are rarely told.
So how then shall we learn?

Gillian Cass

PRECIOUS MOMENTS

Simple things are beautiful, they bring us pleasure
Smiles on children's faces we must always treasure.
Sunbeams bursting through the clouds so dark and grey
Let our hearts be happy, if only for a day.

Raindrops glisten in the sun, after summer showers
Butterflies and bees drink nectar from a feast of flowers.
Gentle breezes blow the cobwebs of a thousand years
Bereavement for a loved one brings so many tears.

A baby being born, their parents full of joy
It matters not if it's a girl or boy.
New life is special for our world to see,
And precious moments must be savoured totally.

Barbara J Hirons

Playing The Numbers Game

There is a big game on Saturday night
Some of the players are relaxed whilst others are uptight
They cannot wait for it to begin
When they all join together hoping to win
There are the 2 fat ladies, 'Dirty Gertie' and 'Droopy Drawers'
Whoever wins gets a big prize and a round of applause
When the game's played, it is as quiet as a mouse
Until, that is, someone shouts, *'House!'*
Because the big game in question
Is not football, rugby or cricket
If you said it was, then they might make a suggestion
As to exactly where you could stick it!
Who knows, they might even try
To punch you in your Kelly's eye
Let me warn you, boy
They will certainly use some fancy lingo
Because it is never a good idea to annoy
The old ladies playing *bingo!*

Russell White

A Sailor's Promise

I'm far at sea
Whilst you're at home
And worry so, when you're alone.

When both of us are far apart
I've always got an aching heart.

For years it's always been like this
A bag on my back and a farewell kiss.

But soon my ship will bring me home
And I'll promise you, I'll never roam
Back on the sea again.

We'll stroll along our usual lane
You and me, and our little girl, Jane.

So with this dove
I've sent my love
Way up high, up in the sky
And over the sea to you.

E V Bowles

You And Only You

You are on my mind day and night
No matter what I do,
I could be out with anyone
But I always think of you.

I don't know what is wrong with me
And why I feel like I do,
You have been in my head
Since the first time I knew you.

At first I didn't think about you
But now I've come to see,
That I really, really like you
Even though you don't like me.

I try to just act normal
But that never seems to work,
As when you're with another girl
All I feel is hurt.

I have tried to just forget you
But you never go away,
I cannot help but wonder
What would happen if I say . . .

'I love you and I have done
Since the first day we met,
Why can't you just realise that
And how could you not know yet?'

I've tried to get you off my mind
But that will never do,
As all it ever comes down to
Is *you* and only *you!'*

Zoe Mellor (14)

CLASSICAL DELIGHTS

(For Ken)

Beethoven, Borodin, Bizet and Britten,
With classical music I'm thoroughly smitten
I listen, enraptured, to the swell of the strings,
The harps and the cellos, the lush violins

The melodious piano absorbs me for hours
The diva soprano, at the height of her powers
The flutes and the oboes - and not to forget
How lovely the sound of the sweet clarinet

A world without music would be no world for me
No thrilling cadenzas in mid-symphony
No lyrical passage to lift up the soul,
Makes for a prospect I've no wish to behold

Elgar, Tchaikovsky, Mozart and Bach,
Over the years, have all made their mark
Driven by genius, their rich legacy,
Food for the spirit and wings to be free.

Brian Ford-Powell

Our Beautiful World

W orld, such a beautiful thing.
Blue, green, countries within.
O r is it just a blob in the sky
lying there waiting to die?
R eady to move near to the sun,
ready to melt, drip down and run.
L onely and bored, no one there.
Then suddenly a rush of people
approaching there.
D elightful world being used and kept
healthy. We are so lucky for this
beautiful planet so wealthy.

Emily Osborne (10)

Experiences Over A Lagoon

After winter, is felt a springtime sensation
Everywhere in the placid silence of the lagoon;
I, along with several others, hired a boat
To enjoy the beauties all about;
The wandering river hesitating,
Flows into the sea straight,
By the freedom of an open horizon;
The boat, drifted by puffs of breeze
Passes swiftly along a broad creek,
Opening out into a wide sweep
Of a stagnant lagoon;
We started very early dawn,
Near the glistening blackness of the water
Here and there, a twisted root of some
Tall tree, writhing and motionless,
Looks like an arrested snake;
Darkness almost oozes out from forests,
Impenetrable and mysterious
Amid the tangled maze of the creepers,
And unstirring fantastic leaves,
Stars seem to have retreated into the frozen
Depths of immense space!
A gust of chill wind stops,
With silence remaining perfect and absolute!
Soon an illumination strange fills
The black and wavy line of forests!
A column of golden light from the sun
Shoots up into the heavens,
And streaks of red-yellow beams,
Create splendour wondrous
Over the semicircle eastern horizon;
The mist breaks into drifting patches,
And the unveiled lagoon lies polished
And black in the heavy shadow of trees;

A white eagle with a slanting and ponderous
Flight, reaches the sunshine clear,
And appears dazzlingly brilliant for the moment;
Then soaring higher, becomes a dark
Motionless speck and into the blue vanishes,
As if it has gone into the heavens
To bring some hopeful bliss for man!

K Ray

Beautiful Things

The world has many beautiful things,
Like diamonds and pearls and golden rings,
There are flowers in bloom, the birds that sing,
And the beloved rose of ours.

There are crystals that shine in the daylight,
And the shimmer of water in the sunlight,
But the most beautiful sight in the world to me,
Is the smile on your face and your heart full of glee.

Constance Cullen

ODD THOUGHTS

The Cornish coast so dangerous and wild,
I well remember as a child.
With legend and mystery in every cave,
The billows, breakers and never-ending wave.

At the height of the storm, when fishing boats shelter,
And fishermen stay beside their hearths so warm,
The gales blow lobster pots a'skelter
Along the quays but cause no harm.

Through the raging storm, return the laden boats.
They were lucky to land their catch
Before the nets were wrested from their grasp.
This shows that the sea had met its match.

Michael John Wilkinson

PROGRESSION

Your soul is on a journey, of this there is no doubt,
The purpose of your time here, is to find what life's about,
Of course you have forgotten what path you should be on
So you must learn and question, to find what must be done.

The beauty all around you, the love that lights your days,
Will help you grow and find yourself in many different ways,
And when this journey's ended, you can go back to the source
For rest and relaxation, until you know your course.

You do not have to come back to this green planet Earth,
There are millions of choices for you to show your worth,
But if you pass and not come back, is truly this your plan?
Then we will miss you as you see, you are part of our clan.

Janet P Higgs

WAR CHILDREN

Through the abandoned streets we run
A horde of children oh so young
Our feet crash down on sand so hard
And a dust cloud rises, yard after yard

The buildings, they stand back to back
And in-between lies an ugly gash
This alley is our chosen home
And here we hide, together alone

We huddle close together now
And our eyes turn to the starry sky
We're thinking of those who offered their arms
In the hope to entice us in

They encircled those arms around us
Sweet warmth so soft and comforting
And the red crosses on their uniforms
Brushed against our skin

But while others let be led away
In the safety of embrace
Some of us could take no more
Of that quiet, beauteous calm

We screamed, we shrieked, we cried like hounds
The pain inside us just as loud
As we battled with our rescuers
Biting their arms till they recoiled from us

Our tiny souls had worn too thin
Like butter over too much bread
Our eyes had now grown cold and dim
And the love within us was dead

But no, I think, in the alley's starlight, remaining in my world so dim
Truth be told, we didn't think anyone could ever love us.

Katie Boyd

The Secret

There is an unknown place of pure, white flowers, flourishing quietly,
Whilst breathing beautiful scents of freedom, unheard,
Where flowering, green lawns surround a calm, still lake.

There is an unknown place, where the delicate blooming of
fresh poppies,
All lie in the wake of endless tranquillity,
Occasionally disturbed by the young birds' songs.

There is an unknown place, of immense peace, pleasure and
infinite joy,
Where the morning dew lies silent, on the crisp grass.
Each blade, a blossoming life of marvel untold,
This, the secret told from young till old.

Gordon Ming-Li Ho

Integrated

I'll take them away those dead metaphors
You hate.
Up, your nose turns at the daily cliché
I offer as your coat and shoes, are removed
At the end of your hardworking day,
I'll stand
Receiving your wares in my inclined hands,
Distant traffic to you, on a road unmanned.

At the door of your study with coffee
I watch.
You place softly your chair with a welcoming cough,
And I drift in my mind and recall
That time,
When the sensitive grasp of your hand carried mine,
And with awe
You told me we fitted like hand into glove,
Now I pick this glove up from the floor.

With dust in my ears I slide into
Your space.
Your screen-focused eyes turn away from my waist,
So I offer my last lead balloon,
Knowing soon
The scent of my pavement will spread through this room,
My voice will fall silent and grey.

So I'll take them away those dead metaphors
You hate.
And our hips playground swings moving forward in space,
I'll untie from their cold rusty cradle,
And saved
From that burden of play, free to strut a new phrase,
You drive off with our rust-seeping trailer.

Donna Maria Fraher

The Prison

This is my prison,
My cell, bound by love.
A love without reasoning,
My inner strength withered.
A shadow of what once was,
Strong woman, vibrant and full.
They take it all, my beautiful children.
The constant bickering, the noise.
I've become so numb to it all.
Like a machine, plug me in, damn it!
Every step forward, such a struggle.
I'm so tired, I could run,
Of course I don't.

My babies need me, I'm a shadow
All sucked out of me, all myself.
Always guilt, give, give, give, until I've nothing left!
Why . . . ? This must be self-abuse . . . because,
One day, to turn and look
Upon an angelic face, bursting with love,
And hope, a sweet smile, and everything . . .
Everything is great, my life's purpose.

Clare Newman

COME IN AT CROW'S-NEST

Different place, different time.
Serving out drinks, to all mankind.
Tall, small, fat and thin.
Let's face it, you can't win.

In they come, one by one.
Eating, drinking as they plod along.
The music is playing, loud and clear.
Someone is celebrating as they all cheer.

So come inside, to our Crow's-Nest
Where we serve you only the best.
Our food is good, rich in taste.
Serving baby courgettes in a savoury paste.

Salmon and caviar in a thick cream sauce,
Digesting, waiting for the second course.
Drink red wine, which tastes so divine.
Or drink white, so clear and bright.

The prices, well, what can I say?
Come inside and see when you pay.
Enter the nest, which is the best
Only you can decide, so give us a test.

Davina Lynn

FREE IS THE EARLY MORNING BREEZE

Free is the early morning breeze,
That twists and turns,
Carefree amongst the trees.

Free is the single raindrop,
Inside a puddle of water,
Free is the man, with no wife,
Son or daughter.

Free is the silence that cannot be kept not heard,
Free is a wild exotic bird.

Free is the rainbow,
That disperses each of its colours,
Free is a life,
Amongst the fullest.

Nardeen Némat

A Strange Sight

I saw an ant swallow a whale
    I saw a strange tiger without a tail
I saw a frog play a drum
    I saw a fly chew some gum
I saw a rabbit that changed to a hare
    I saw a lion go to the fair
I saw a parrot peck a head
    I saw a fly that was being fed
I saw a girl change to a male
    I saw a snake go for a sail.

Katie Elizabeth Shaw (9)

Notes From A Confined Life

Milepost

The night comes slowly
Each moment falling gently
As a petal shed in summer stillness
The tide of light receding without notice
Long closed up is dandelion's face
And insects hide in leafy shelter
The blackbird's singing fades, note by note
And soon is lost in dusk's advancing cloak.
I close the curtain, absorbing peace
Another day's end is safely reached.

Passing thoughts

Heartless sun! How can you shine
When burdens of this world oppress us?
Skies turn to rain and wash away
The heavy load of our despair

Action pending

The afternoon lies heavy and quiet
The trees skeletal
A single leaf, not quite loosening its precarious hold
Moves gently with the air's soft breath
A light shines briefly in a distant window
No one crosses the field
The backdrop hill is darker still than leaden sky.
The window frame's a theatre set
But when will the play begin?

A balancing act

All the tears of this sad world
Would fill a vast deep ocean
All its joys a wide blue sky,
Pray that in the space between
We share in both before we die.

Marjorie Lloyd

TALE OF THE ENGLEWOOD FAIRIES

One fine day in summertime,
in a town not so far away,
in the enchanted forest of Englewood,
the fairies come out to play.

When people are finished dreaming,
in the time between sleep and awake,
when the moon is a distant shadow,
and the darkness begins to break.

Deep in the heart of the forest,
alongside a silver stream,
although the forest is silent,
things are not quite what they seem.

As the minutes count down to morning,
and the air is filled with a glow,
the forest is coated in golden dust,
and the fairies begin to show.

Fairies come from all over,
to take part in this event,
together they join in song and dance,
just as Heaven had meant.

When the party has nearly ended,
and the night given way to the sun,
the fairies begin to disappear,
coating the plants one by one.

Now you have heard my tale of the fairies,
but if you don't believe what you hear,
why not come down to the Englewood forest,
they will be here the same time next year.

Lauren Taaffe (15)

My Grandad's Sweater

If I'm not feeling very well,
There's only one thing that can make me better,
I think you know!
Do you know?
Well, shall I tell you?
It's my grandad's woolly sweater.

It's woolly and cuddly and very soft,
I haven't seen it much these days,
It's hiding in the loft.
It's never, never wet,
And it's never, never sticky (like a toffee),
And it's never, never stinky,
Like my dad's coffee.

There's nothing that can make me better
More than my grandad's woolly sweater.

Chloë Ward

METEOR

Zzoomsh! It burst through the sky wielding a mighty flame
Licking the air whilst screeching its name to them that looked on
The lingering horrid sight given by those who dared to glimpse
A terrific boom as the ground gulped the huge crash,
instant catastrophe!

It was too late and doom had already booked its place
The sea bellowed its breath into the sky then drew again in chaos
No last stand for all those living that tried to shield and
Nothing spared as Mother Nature brutally lashes her dear child

Nobody here now, only a stillness so great, so vast, so empty.
Importance still breathes but what will they do now?
Irony laughs at them and they knew all along, everything, ever since
The war started, the war against nature.

That dark blanket waves goodbye to the light, and the light sleeps.
A promise delivered from the dawn of time, with an unchanged gift.
Some day the darkness will pass into history, a long wait
Then they'll finally see from where it was they came.

Jason Farrell

HOLD TIGHT!

When your sanity is wavering over the edge
And you find yourself teetering on a ledge
You are not alone in despair, I can confess
For I too have fought my way back from stress

Open your eyes and see life's medicine before you
It can come in the shape of a friend strong and true
Who's ready to drag you from the depths of Hell
The deep dark pit into which you find you've fell

Churchill named his as a dog always ready to follow
But fight it, my friend, and in it don't stop and wallow
Find your salvation, be it in music, or a walk at dawn
Playing sport, or the simple pleasure of a summer's morn.

Many find it too easy to hit the self-destruct key
Life's a gift, an adventure, worth the travelling, you will see
For if you can conquer the black clouds hanging over you
Then time will show the golden rainbow coming from the blue.

Jeannie Ashplant

NONENTITY

I am the foetus
In the jar,
Aware,
Cast adrift,
Too far,
No hope of rescue,
A floating soul,
An exhibit,
A view,
Without a goal,
A second's passion,
Then there was me,
An appendage,
For eternity.

Polly Pawson

Our Nana

(Read at the funeral of Mrs Alexcina Hermel, 6th July 2004)

Our nana was such a caring lady who was loved so very much
She showed this through her gentle smile and her gentle touch
She thought about us every day of every single year
And now we're finding it really hard not to shed a tear
We know she wouldn't want us to, so we shall try to be strong
But we are not entirely sure how long that can go on

We know she will be sadly missed by all her family and friends
But this doesn't have to mean that all her life's come to an end
For she lives on in all of us through our memories so dear
And if we look at them closely enough they will become quite clear.

We know she's up there at this moment looking down on us
Wondering why on earth we're making all this fuss
For she would have been quite happy to slip away quietly
And have her ashes sprinkled round a very beautiful tree

So Nana, we'd like to say 'Goodbye' and wish you all the best
For now you are in Grandad's arms so together you may rest.

Lee Hermel

BATS

As I sit and watch the bats by night
I watch through the window, with terrible fright
They fly around above the ground
Silently without a sound

Black as black
They whiz straight past
Flying, flying
Very fast.

Chasing each other
With the greatest of ease
In and out
The apple trees.

Within 20 minutes
They have gone
Right back home
Where they belong.

Lorraine Woodgate

WORRIED

Please can you tell me
I'm getting rather sad
I keep sending you poems
Are they all that bad?
I used to get in print
Every poem as I recall
Now it seems
You don't need them at all!
Please can you tell me
My memory is hazy
Are they not up to standard
Or am I just getting lazy?

Rowena Haley

WENCH'S DILEMMA

A prince's gift, some do say
10 guineas and a promise
The lasting favour of the crown
And a lifetime's honour

For just one night of love's unrest
A wench's maiden given
A tumble of the even kind
With ecstasy delivered

What future mine should I
Decline to take this generous offer
No food for me or home I'll see
If virgin pride prevails

And ruin yet to then accept
Mine only crown be foiled
Along with life as some man's wife
For who takes a maiden soiled.

Susie Powell

French Kiss

It was a wink, a curtain call, a fall.
Like tying a knot with gloved hands.
A girl on a beige bed, a boy by the wall.
I sang while you kissed me,
ardent, not for you, but that final note
that, when it came, poured from my throat
in a honeyed rush.

It was a hovering, a seamless act, a pact
but you held me and struggled
against the weight of a thousand, the cold fact.
I smiled and I soothed and I bore
your reference in bravado to the girl before,
a different life.

It was a plague, a wound, rigidity assumed.
The room made new as before.
Lives I never led mercifully presumed.
But surely you knew from the way
my tongue fled in my mouth and beyond?
The voidable bond.

Catherine Boal

Chop Suey Rolls

You never quite know what's inside
this long tube of fried batter,
but once you've got your chops round one
it doesn't really matter.

Rip it all to pieces
with your jagged teeth.
Pull the stringy insides out
and suck it underneath.

Lynne Dwyer

The Wicked Witch

The wicked witch of the north came down
Flying on her broomstick all around
Casting a spell on anyone in town
All in black with a velvet gown

The wicked witch with her pointed black hat
Sat on her broomstick with her black cat
Thinking of potions for girls and boys
And anyone else who dares make a noise

The wicked witch on her broomstick flies
Over the hills and up in the skies
Going back home now Hallowe'en has been
She did not see us but she was seen

The wicked witch was seen up high
Flying past the moon way up in the sky
She's going home, we all cheer
Now she has gone for another year.

P R Ward

MANDY'S COTTAGE

There's a quaint little cottage,
Beside a cool stream,
Where birds sing so sweetly,
And wildflowers dream.
There's a yellow-gold field
Stretching out into space,
And a feeling of peace
In this fairy-tale place.
When the moon fills the sky -
As it peeps through the trees -
Not a sound can be heard
But the whispering breeze.
Here's a little dog barking
As he runs around,
Trying to tell you
Of bones he has found.
You feel closer to God,
In the wild of the land,
For you hold paradise -
In the palm of your hand.
There's a quiet little cottage
In a sweet lovely dell,
With an air of contentment
You can't buy or sell.

Mavis Green

The Lost Child

Upon this earth so cold and grey
A child lies cryin', 'I've lost my way'
He says with a heart, broken and torn
Eyes full of mud, his soul has been worn

Away from the pain, the anger, the hate
He tries to crawl but is held down by fate
With no more strength he slowly gives in
And asks for absolution from his only sin,

To be alive and to walk on this damned Earth,
But now he realises that his life was not worth
The suffering and hurt his loved ones endured
To make sure this worthless boy's life was ensured

As he slowly fades into the dark angel's hands
The pain and suffering he now understands
That death is beauty that cannot be seen
And the end we all suffer and it does not justify the means.

Summer Lili

Winter Days

The days are getting shorter,
Not so long is the light
The wind it grows colder
As the day turns into night

The trees are changing colour
From lush green to brown,
And then they drop their withered leaves
Onto the cooling ground

The flowers wither up now
Back into the earth
Waiting for next springtime
For their rebirth

Soon there will be snow now,
Right outside the door,
This will be the winter snow,
Like we had before.

Michael Scott

Lovely Morning

The early morning mists hides in the shadows
Hovering over the murky canal
The heron stooped like an old man
Waits for his breakfast near an old tin can
Some ducks warm themselves in the first rays of sun
A dog cocks his leg waiting for his owner to come

A bleary-eyed man ambles to work thinking of last night
Was she really so lovely? Was she really worth a fight?
The roar of the main road beckons
As he climbs the slope from peace and quiet
Puffing and blowing, 'I really should go on a diet'

The shattered glass in the shelter lies all around
Like hundreds of diamonds on a deserted beach waiting to be found
Glistening in the sunshine as it crackles underfoot
Another mess for someone to clear
Caused by a drunken boot

Along the street past the overflowing bins
To work again for his sins
As he wanders through the foyer
Shirt untucked, still yawning
The irritating over-friendly receptionist greets him
'What a lovely morning!'

Andrew Sulman

True Love

All that has life in this fair land
Has need to think, to discover
How to mate with another
'Tis built in and planned
Flowers, with colour scent the air
Hungry wings, know just where
Scent, is the guide for all
Fish brave high waters
For their kind to be born
Leaving eggs to hatch
With food, they can catch
Some species, only breed
Giving only their seed
Seeing not, the wonders
Nor feeling, the unseen
On land, and yonder above
Called love, is this feeling
So appealing, this love.

H Cotterill

WAITING

More than time is a measure,
Love alters an eye faster than eternity.
She appetites in a sea of hearts
Efficiently as a rose in summer's breath,
Where minds are an ocean of dreams
Between sunset and sunrise.
Her chance to survive in the forest of night,
Reaches from star to star
Quicker than a journey, distanced
On a drawn line before the now and there.
But love is a fill,
Surplus to the air that surrounds her kiss
And time is a hope,
Equal in measure
For those prepared to wait.

Christopher W Wolfe

Old Monterey

When evening falls in Monterey
And twilight tiptoes softly down,
Across the avenues of night
Where quiet haciendas lay,
A myriad twinkling stars look down
On ornate fountains as they play.

Desert orchid, cactus rose,
Embrace the night in sweet repose,
Whilst up on high a moon so bright
Reveals the beauty with its light.

Ernest Clinton Jones

16th July 1977 - Kris's Birthday

Your birth date was important;
Confirmation of a plan.
God marked you out and chose you,
Before the world began.

New songs are being written
And sung for all to hear,
Just take the stage; we'll listen for
You're going up a gear.

This year is most significant,
Quite soon you will know why,
Important that you listen,
And remember to aim high.

Now share a time of laughter
Light-heartedness and fun,
This new year stretched before you,
Has only just begun!

Today, right now, enjoy it
And have a lovely day,
Old promises will be fulfilled,
Touch keys and start to play.

Gillian Humphries

Bye . . .

This is my boundary
There is no way forward.

I take the knife to my throat,
The blade gleaming in the dark.

I carve an intense line,
The blood starts flowing rapidly.

I stare as the pool becomes deeper
And more deadly.

This is my way.
No one can terminate this.

I feel my life being extracted from me,
It's starting to become impossible to breathe.

I only have a few seconds to live,
My eyes are starting to decease.

Bye to all those who say they love me,
But lie.

Bye . . .

Clare Gollop

United

We're the same,
yet we're different in similar ways.
Our forefathers walked apart
but today we walk side by side.
Many don't understand the way they feel,
but there are others who ignore
the barriers that have formed.
The land is crumbling into
disarray and mayhem.
But even as we fight,
we stand together united as one.

Gemma Mountain

The Skeleton Standing In The Sea

For a moment
I just sat there
staring at the rusty iron structure
wind blowing through my hair
years ago she was a fine-looking lady
not today
those looks have long gone away
'Will she be restored?' I hear you say.
Maybe, someday.

For years
the birds have made it their home
gathering early evenings
for a chat, a laugh, for a singsong
thousands following their leader's every move
silhouetting against the sunset
getting into the groove.

Piers,
once there were two
not now
this one has burnt right through
decayed and rusted
through all of the years
people sit outside the bars on the seafront
chilling and drinking their beers
watching, staring
at the skeleton in the sea
once majestic, so powerful
now just a broken old lady
people reminisce of times gone by
a seagull stands on the pebbles
with tears in its eyes.

So to the future
does anybody really know?
Many locals saying
'Nothing will happen'
and 'Yes, we told you so'.
Is it a loss or is there a chance the remainder won't fall
or will we still be wondering
reading the writing on the wall . . . ?

Stephen A Owen

BROKEN HEART

My garden was the haven where Shannon and I - on sunny days -
Scattered hopeful seeds to the winds.
Now the blessed flowers are all I have
To remind me of this golden angel of a rose.
The ambling walks by shaded trees
Searching for frogs after summer showers.
Clutching bluebells close to our hearts
Wistful tiny hand enveloped in mine.
This thin and bruised body sustained by me
Often wracked with sobs, tiny chest heaving.
Cocooned in a warm and loving blanket.
Coaxing morsels into bird-like mouth,
Keeping voice gentle to soften her face.
Looming away so as not to see her frightened wide-eyed wince.
This angel, whose mother now has chosen her way out
To pursue her never-ending quest.
This child, whose life has parted from mine
In case - she remembers.

Carolyn Attfield

EASTER IN SPRINGTIME

How lovely is springtime,
It's like a fresh start,
And nature, as always, is playing her part.
Our winter blues have been despatched,
Now fluffy yellow chicks are being hatched.
The golden primroses are having their say,
Smiling up through the grass
To brighten our day.
And the trees that for months,
Have stood gaunt and bare,
Are showing new green leaves to wear.
So we say, welcome to the spring,
And the joys of Easter,
And all Easter brings.
Our first holiday of the year,
To relax and have fun.
To indulge in chocolate eggs,
And hot cross buns.

D Morris

A Peek At Life

Fields full of buttercups, cowslips like lace
Walk through them now at a very slow pace
Make a picture at the back of your mind
Then try to explain it to someone who's blind

A walk in the country, a stroll in the park
We take it for granted, it's never too dark.

Terence Payne

FREYA

I went to Great Yarmouth
For a midsummer holiday
To see my sister Debbie,
Also Siobhan and Deb's new love, David, hey!

I rode the Bure Valley Railway
But upon the longest day,
The weather turned evil and wet
Not a typical summer's day.

But on Friday I saw baby Freya
With her mummy, Deb, in Yarmouth
Friday, some say, is Freya's day
Norse God of Love, no doubt.

H G Griffiths

INVITATION TO A WEDDING OF SORTS

Could this not be one of many an ancient curse?
Clearly mythic, never a genuine, polite invite
To a wedding, perhaps to some kind of pagan rite,
Topics devout clerics may well wish to discuss.
On receipt of one's summons to the future nuptials
Between Otto Carr and spinster, Anne Omnibus,
RSVP, will be both courteous and highly desirous,
If attending such marriage signing-on contractuals.
Wedding breakfast, after, courtesy of Anchor Books.
Photos to be seen within future issues of Poetry Now,
If not, then maybe published in an anthology somehow,
Although editors may doubtless monitor how awful it looks.
All subsequent warfare is now known as marital strife.
What kind of fool would take Anne Omnibus for a wife?

Anne Omnibus

I Made It Rain

Imagine a life too good to be true,
everything you want, belonging to you,
walking around with a smile on your face,
feeling happy, feeling in place.
The sun shining on you wherever you go,
you're so happy, everyone should know,
feeling secure, happy and sane,
I had that once, but I made it rain.

Learn to love the life you have got,
stop wanting more 'cause you will lose the lot,
take a step back and watch for a while,
you have more than some people, but they still smile.
Enjoy every minute, live life to the full,
be a great person, don't be a fool,
don't lose what you have, don't suffer the pain,
like I did that day, when I made it rain.

Hayley Kinnaird

The Seasons Of My Soul

In acquiescing unto you
My petals wax and wane
I blossom in our spring
Then when it's cold I die again.
Blooms of blood-red roses
Diminish by my side
Weary from the darkness
And damaged by the lies.

Summertime luminescence reigns
My heart sees brighter days
But when the wind turns colder
Love's young dream decays
Resounding sentiments of hate
Then soulful pleas for pardon
Petals descend and putrefy
Lamenting in my garden

The autumn winds and winter skies
Arrest my spirit risen
There is no place for flowers now
In this domestic prison
This rose unfolds and withers
No further blooms to give
Exquisite but ever transient
There's no more life to live.

Hannah Pay

Black

Dirty coal smudged on a smoky chimney,
Darkness filling the air full of evil breeze,
Like a cold, lonely, eerie room.
Dark in the galaxy where planets begin to freeze,
Dusk returning, sunlight fading.
Nothing but emptiness like the fearless ocean.
A shadow lurking in the distance, far and near,
The cavernous sea so vast and open.

Michael Man & Gordon Ho

SALVATION

Want to become a child of God?
This is what you say aloud:
'Father God
I ask this in the name of Jesus
I'm sorry for my sin, please forgive me
I ask you, Jesus, to come into my life
I believe in my heart
And confess with my mouth,
That You are my Lord and Saviour
From this moment on I will follow You
Thank You for saving me now
And making me a child of Yours
I am saved
Amen.'

Berenice Healy

AMBITIONS

One day when a youngster so full of ambition,
I made up my mind that I'd conquer the world.
Didn't know how I'd manage, but knew I must do it.
The flag of my heart must be truly unfurled.
I tried and I tried, but I met with frustration,
For patience, I had none to meet with the task.
My mother and father they told me to slow down
They'd help me for sure - I had only to ask.

But deep independence prevented me asking,
And I all alone my ambition pursued.
Frustration grew deeper, no progress encountered,
And deep disappointment forever ensued.
By now my tenth birthday was looming much closer,
And still I was seeking to know what to do.
And then on my birthday, a book I was given -
I found it was aptly entitled, 'Who's Who'.

So I read this book about those who'd succeeded,
Discovered that none of them struggled alone;
They asked help from others whose lives they admired,
From those who had shared with them all that they'd done.
I knew as I read it that others could help me
To reach my ambition, I swallowed my pride,
And asked those around me who knew more than I did
To help me, be with me, and walk by my side.

I'm not now a youngster, but still have ambition,
(I know that I'll never now conquer the world.)
Just living my life in the way of the Saviour -
The flag of my heart has been truly unfurled.
And now I've reached sixty and life's full of blessings,
I have one ambition that's deep in my heart,
That I may be used by my dear Lord and Saviour,
To all that I meet God's great love to impart.

Anne Gray

Reflections Of Cape Town, South Africa

Emerging on the horizon from our ocean liner
Appeared a new land incomparable and finer
Residing amidst exotic wildlife all around
The magnificence of which never failed to astound

Looking in awe at the miles of golden sands
Glistening and slipping like silk through our hands
The majestic Table Mountain standing proud
Appearing mysterious draped with swirling mist and cloud

The glorious radiant sun and luminous skies of blue
And picturesque skyline encompassing beauty so true
Mountainous panorama enveloped by fresh exhilarating air
Displaying exquisite wild flowers growing so rare

Blissful sumptuous days then drew to an end
Our broken hearts we did endeavour to mend
An enchanting country we'd tried hard to understand
The political complexities of this truly idyllic land.

Julia Keiser

Lowestoft

The eastern coast is brisk and fresh; the air is rarely mild,
the sea is deep and dark and brown, the waves are rough and wild.

It doesn't make you want to swim and frolic in its depths,
you'll be content to walk along with careful steady steps.

The pebbles strewn about the beach will make a crunching sound,
they're all so smooth and soft and sleek and uniformly round.

You pick one up and throw it far into the waves so high,
your gaze goes up and lingers where the sea meets with the sky.

It really is quite lovely here, not peaceful that is true,
but beautiful and free and wild, a stunning sight to view.

Muriel Nicola Waldt

Walk On By

When you see a drunk in the street
When you see a dying man's heart beat
When traitors spy
When politicians lie
    Walk on by
When you see brave men try
When you see kids die
When you see women cry
When you see the missiles fly
    Walk on by
No more heroes anymore!

John McCartney

HEAVENLY LIGHT

When the toils of day
Have passed away
One seeks the heavenly light
That shines so bright

From thy heart a little prayer
With the Holy One in power
When thou feel uplifted
Thy heart spiritually healed

Seeking at night the sky above
Thou feel such love
Many twinkling stars shine so bright
For a moment one feels in flight

With feelings serene
Whisked away in a pleasant dream
Feeling renewed the morrow
Accepting whate'er may follow

When thy spirit feels low
A prayer gives thee a glow
And a heavenly sense of sanctuary
Where'er thou be

Given to prayer at night
Brings heavenly light
Taking away all sorrow
Giving strength for the morrow.

Josephine Foreman

The Rainbow

There it was in the sky,
As bright as the sun in my eyes.

It stretched across the whole wide world,
I loved the way the rainbow curled.

I would like some of the unicorns there,
I have read about them, they are very rare.

A rainbow is magical in its own way,
I would like to get the pot of gold at the end of it
Some day.

Kamini Manivasagam (11)

Africa!

Africa! Africa! The mother of civilisation
In thy bosom many have schooled
But now a land forgotten by time
Like Rome to Greece
The captive has captured the captor

Africa! Africa! Treasure base of mankind
In thy coffers many are made great
Yet you beg to live
And like the notorious Oliver Twist
Always asking for more

Africa! Africa! The citadel of potentials
Great and able hands thou hast produced
But expertise though now seeketh in the land of the white
Like a male seeking female company
Yet with abundance females in his pad

Africa! Africa! An icon of unity
Peace and equality thou hast advocated
But here you are fragmented by ethnic clashes
Like the renowned preacher
Do what I say and not what I do!

Africa! Africa! The home of all
In thee God dwells
In thee the Devil reigns
Tell me, where is the hope Mother Africa?
In life or in life after death?

Mfon Michael Essien

Dying

I'm dying for a cigarette
To fill my lungs with tar.
Add poisons to my bloodstream
And cough up black catarrh.

I'm dying for a drag or puff -
Shorten my life expectancy.
Die of cancer, clog up my heart
Or some statistical fatality.

I'm dying for a long, cool lug
To calm my nerves, to feed my habit,
I need to breathe in toxic fumes,
How long can my body stand it?

I'm dying for my hourly fag
Fill my airway up with smoke.
I'd go to great lengths for a drag
Even though I'm broke!

I can't give up, I'm hooked, I'm weak,
The future for me is so bleak,
I'm not quite ready to quit just yet.
I'm dying from a cigarette.

Linda Lawrence

TRAINS

Walked briskly, set off in high glee
going on holiday today, as you can see.
Going on a train for the very first time
with Mum and Dad,
Talking and laughing on the way.

Listen to the wheels go clickety-clack
dimly lit carriages, a whistle blowing
on a mysterious train.
Taking me to a wondrous place,
Mum said, 'We're all going on a steam train
which goes around the place.'

When I'm all grown up, I will be
a station master, just like my dad.

A Shedlow

YOUR MISTRESS

You have loved me more than any man
I have ever known,
The times you took my breath away
and I took yours.
A mystery man when we first met,
an enigma with friends, yet alone.

I watched you a million times, whilst you were preoccupied,
what was on your mind?
Wondering what deep secret encased you -
the key I had to find.

Your faithfulness was tested to a fine degree,
your loyalty was tested too with fire and water.
What was wrong with me?

While delving one day in the chasms of your mind,
you smiled and made me laugh, what a trick!
Your restless soul I could not appease
you needed another sip.

One was too many, a million not enough,
you hated every bubble but you still drank and drank.
Helplessly I had to watch as my rival took my man.

As I go to the hospital to pick up your clothes
my life in total distress.
What pride can I feel, being the love of your life
when the bottle was your mistress.

A Hyde Murphy

Fête Accompli

It's no surprise to me to learn
That charity is rife in Herne
With kisses costing ten pence each
And fun and games along the beach.

There's fancy cakes and objets d'art
Which sometimes seem a bit bizarre
There's horticultural prizes too
With sizes to astonish you!

And lots of undiscovered talent
Suddenly becomes apparent
With pastimes that defy convention
But are not lacking in invention!

And you are there to see it works
And duff up anyone who shirks.
Dear organiser rest a while
And count the takings with a smile.

A toast to you and one and all,
But pass the bottle before you fall.
Emotions now are so intense -
Have a peanut and hang the expense!

Betty Nevell

Meeting Venus

Letting her tunic fall on the strand,
the love goddess sought approval: ‘And?’

Unsure if he was dreaming or not,
the young sailor just wondered, ‘And what?’

That left the goddess to take the lead,
which she did with an ‘And what indeed!’

Richard John Lewis

Whispers

Whispers, too many whispers.
Listen!
Whispers carried by the summer breeze
Through the trees and streams, can you hear?
Hazy days, memories, voices
In whispers.
Plato's prisoners, chained into the darkness of the cave
Are we brave in shadowland, second-hand
Experiences, eyes closed, who knows
If we are blind?
Sunshine, night-time, blinding, reminding us
Of the whispers carried by the summer breeze
Forcing us onto our knees in submission
To the condition of life.

Elaine Pomm

Moments

Bat flies, won't lose moth,
Slowly, slowly, catch the moth.
Moth not hidden by the night's black cloth.
Ducks from bat - clever moth.

Red-breasted robin chirps happily.
Challenges blue tit - sings happily.
Robin smiles, eats bug snappily.
Search for mate completed happily.

The raven splodges to the ground,
Messy fight, high from ground.
Raven's eyes, big and round,
Feeling sick, stuck on ground.

Cows in field, chomp all day.
Wander, mooing in field today.
Whilst horses chomp and guzzle hay
The cows munch grass (or milk) all day.

Seagulls soar, and dive for fish.
Gliders soar, no dive for fish.
Copy seagulls, might fly by wish.
Seagulls swallow scaly fish.

Rats creep round to find next meal
Rabbit, sewage or mice for meal.
Always sneak, sneak and steal.
Constantly wonder - my next meal?

Housefly zooms, escaping storm
Ferociously windy thunderstorm.
Blown around, not in good form,
Gonna be beaten by the storm.

All these creatures in a moment,
All been caught in a moment.
All of these a small component
On the Earth, each unique moment . . .

Sarah Moran (15)

ON THE WINDOW SILL

How I came to be here I don't know,
but now that I am here, will I grow?
Am I a flower or am I a tree?
I'm confused, so will you please tell me.

Out of the window I can look
And I'm watching you writing in that book,
I try to ask you (are you writing about me?)
and if so, am I a flower or a tree?

You look at me but give no reply
Why won't you answer me, why oh why?
It's cloudy outside and I can see some rain
Please don't put me out there again.

Over towards me I watch you walk
But it's no good, you can't hear me talk.
You speak to me so lovingly
I can hear you, so why can't you hear me?

I watch you turn the tap on at the sink,
Are you going to be kind and give me a drink.
Thank you, thank you, that's lovely
I'm sure that time you really heard me.

When I came here I was small and weak
Now I'm getting stronger, week by week.
You do a good job of looking after me
But I still don't know if I'm a flower or a tree!

I sit here and watch you come and go
And watch you watching me, slowly grow
You might think I'm a silly flower or tree
Well you look even sillier to me.

Remember I watch you in the mornings drink your tea
And remember I can hear you but you can't hear me.
I don't care if I'm a flower or a tree
I'm glad to be here and just to be me.

Dereck Palmer

WHATEVER HAPPENED TO . . . ?

Whatever happened to our country, a Nation we were?
Whatever happened to our young people, who do not care?
Whatever happened to our houses, we have none?
Whatever happened to our schools, closing one by one?
Whatever happened to our hospitals, have no beds?
Whatever happened to our police, has no head?
Whatever happened to our army, gone abroad?
Whatever happened to our churches, where's God?
Whatever happened to charity, not at home?
Whatever happened to our pensioners, all alone?
Whatever happened to peace, went astray?
Whatever happened to our leaders, lost their way?

So what happens now?

Robert Henry

The Desert

The desert lies still and dead
As the sun goes by,
The sun shines, yellow and red,
You can hear the valleys sigh.

The wild kookaburra sings
Into the deep, dark night,
You can hear the flapping of wings,
As the birds are in mid-flight.

The drooping mugga-wood tree
Has puce coloured flowers,
It shows the opposite to glee
And may have very strange powers.

The scorching desert waits
With its water-filled billabongs,
It is in the hands of fate
If in the desert, you live long.

Vinothini Manivasagam

Mrs Learie

My eleventh grade teacher wept with raw emotion
when reciting a passage from Harper Lee's novel.
She had taught the same syllabus for the duration of her career
yet still the words touched her as fresh as they did on the initial read.

I listened to every word and quiver in her throat.
The only other time I'd seen her cry
was when her father unexpectedly died.
Only this time I wanted to be her.

She taught me well; the structure, the grammar,
Poetry and prose, the correct language to use.
But more than this she evoked the soul
and showed me how literature was composed
in order to unfreeze hearts, both weary and cold.

Rebecca Connery

Love Changes Me Indeed!

I may have waited many years but it was really worth the wait.
I've just learned that I am truly loved and no longer live with hate.
'Tis just now I have become aware love was always there for me.
Love chose this time to reveal himself, 'tis the time to set me free.
Now free I am and overjoyed, all the lies I leave behind.
My life is now a rainbow because love has changed my mind
All glory, laud and honour to thee.

Rosie Hues

The Mystic

No time . . . no distractions
no befores . . . no afters
no thoughts of any kind

motionless he kneels
and with eyes closed
leaves the world behind

and leaves his image
stamped upon my mind.

Fay Smith

I'M NOT LIKE EVERYONE ELSE

I'm not like everyone else,
I don't have a strong sense of self,
I feel like everyone's staring at me,
I'm just like them, can't they see?
Don't they know it's the inside you count,
Because inside I have a large amount.
Just because I have no hair,
Just because I use a wheelchair.
Other people can be what they want to be,
Things I can't do because of my disability.
Some people are lucky they've only got spots,
But everyone who looks can tell what I've got.
There are lots of things I can't do,
Even if I wanted to.
I can't be a teacher or a ballet dancer,
Because, alas, I've got cancer.

Melissa Shepherd (12)

My Garden

My garden is so beautiful
I created it myself.
It's warm, it's cosy - somewhere to lose yourself.

I don't know what all my flowers are
Called - and don't really care - you see
Within my garden, the peace of God is
There.

Butterflies come, butterflies go,
Insects take their time.
Bees buzz to and fro
Slugs eat what they can
I'm so happy with my garden
And don't really care.
My garden is so beautiful -
I'm happy there.

I'm in my garden every day,
I watch new flowers born,
They bloom, they make me happy
Still I don't really care - you see
It's my garden and I'm peaceful,
My heart, my soul are there.

Helen Dakin

The Potted Cactus

I wish I were home in the desert, a place of constant delight
where the sun rises high in the morning
and dives into bright stars at night
I wish I were home in the desert
a land so rare and so bright
with silica showers and dunes and dunes
occasional flowers like us, which bloom
I wish I were home in the desert
again, again and again.

Mac Westland

The Intrepid Snail

The wallflowers thought that they were safe on high
But reckoned without the snail so sly
He had woken up from his sleep
Thought he might just take a peek
At the little green plants above his head
But what he saw filled him with dread
Could he climb to the mountain top?
Would he get part way, then have to stop?

For on a table on the patio stood
The precious plants to newly bud
He took a chance and climbed up the table side
As he reached the top he beamed with pride
But to his dismay the plants were in a large tray
He sighed, surely I haven't come all this way
To fail and not get a little taste
All this energy gone to waste.

He thought I'll give it one more try
His motto was to do or die
Perseverance was his name
He knew this might be his only claim to fame
As he grew nearer, the wallflowers cried out in terror
The gardener had made a terrible error
For the snail now in earnest was munching away
A nice choice breakfast he was having today.

Josephine R Banks

My Garden

The season gardener may come and go
pulling their hair out and tugging their hoe.

Dreading the weeds and pleasing the flowers
they sit in the garden for hours and hours.

The teacup is empty, work must begin
I need to get on with this enormous thing.

Every day is such a race, working in
such a space.

Will it go this way, will it go there?
I put it in and stop and stare.

Moulding, caressing, pleasing, suggesting,
listening, smelling and digesting!

At the end of it all, I sit and contemplate
will this ever work?

To mix flowers, vegetables, wildlife alike,
I gaze at it all,
It's such a delight.

Sally Cocking

Wenche's Garden

A little plot, only twelve yards by ten
Blooms and herbs inter-planted. Tall and small
Vegetables, fruit and shrubs, it's got them all
Has my friend Wenche's hard-working garden.
On a pocket handkerchief of a lawn
We bask in the sunshine all summer long
Eating home-made scones with jam made from fruit
Grown in Wenche's garden, last autumn's loot.
Drinking endless cups of Earl Grey tea
Studying the progress of buzzing bees
Tumbling and bumbling gold and black shower.
Drunk on the heady potpourri perfumes
Issuing from the multicoloured blooms
Make mem'ries to last till my dying hours.

T M Garfield

Pick Me While I Am A Rose

Pick me while I am a rose
Before my petals die away,
Red and sweet they bloom today
In deep and velvet hue

Pick me while my potent scent
Intoxicates with heady glow,
Seduction is its purpose now
With fragrant, honeyed dew

Pick me while my pollen clouds
In yellow dust before your eyes,
Enticing you, with wanton sighs,
To make me all your own.

One day I will shed my gown
My crimson raiment fade and wilt
Tarnished jewels, strewn and spilt,
From summer's ruby crown.

Brenda Maple

Goodbye Again

(For Amanda)

So here we are at the end of our time,
Inexorably drawing us on,
Into the void of being apart.
In moments, your bus will have come and gone.

I cannot reveal or describe how I feel,
For to tell you would be too high a cost.
I stand here alone, refugee-like, no home,
Like a little boy helpless and lost.

Our goodbye embrace and the wide crowded space,
Into infinity stretches for ever.
Asking you when will I see you again?
I fear you will answer with never!

I'm walking away, with so much to say,
The words simply pound in my head,
The grey afternoon of unending gloom,
Heralds solitude laden with dread.

And so, you've gone home and I'm standing alone,
Like a castaway pacing the shore,
Watching the gulls as they wheel in the sun,
Hearing the sea's mighty roar.

I gaze from life's beach, as the Kittiwakes screech,
And the tide washes over the stones,
But wherever you go,
My darling, you'll know
I am with you, you are never alone.

Keith William Hewett

A Peaceful Summer Scene

Summer and the black crows flew in a flock
Over the green branches of the tall pine trees
A dotting of white clouds scurried across the sky
'But enough blue to make a sailor's shirt'
Commented one visitor treading the path carefully
And others looked up and smiled.
Everyone had high hopes that
The weather was set fair for a special day.

The festival taking place in the woods,
Roman invasion, a touch of history
The mystery and fascination of the past.
Enacted out in a sandy clearing with noise,
Confusion and good humoured laughter.
The young ones were getting into the spirit of things,
And their parents were quietly watching the struggle
To dress for battle in a complicated costume.
Roman General resplendent and ready for the fray
Waiting patiently.

Further away on a high path among the pines
A carved wooden figure seated on a bench
Provided rest for a mum as her two children
Rushed between trees doing a treasure hunt for a prize.
There was a patient smile in her eyes,
Moment of family history recorded by their dad's camera.

Freda Grieve

The Excavators

On moorland,
Where the lonely curlew cries across the heath
Where only scattered bloom
Of tormantil, or prickly gorse or broom,
Relieve the wasteland stretched before the eyes.
The stones of an ancient burial chamber rise
Above on earthen mould and
In this tomb,
Ranged like an unborn infant in the womb,
The proud dust of a warrior Chieftain lies.
I think they laid him thus within the earth,
In hope that faith and magic enterprise,
Would win his infant soul a heavenly birth,
Perhaps they hymned his deeds to former skies.
Hoping the listening Gods would praise his worth and
We who dig him out, are no more wise.

H Scatchard

A Sailor's Nightmare

Floating silently across the water,
destruction in its path,
taking boats and ships from the ocean top,
down to their deep blue grave.

Floating silently across the water,
it's every sailor's nightmare
to come face to face with a jagged mass of ice
from which there is no escape.

Floating silently across the water,
showing no signs of mercy,
the iceberg carves its way through the waves
towards the next victim.

Kim Gower

A Yellow Daffodil

Announcing the approach of spring,
pushing through the hardened clay,
I am a yellow daffodil fed by winter's long decay.

Linda Kay Mottet

Born During The War

I was born during the war
So a lot of money we never saw
Our fun had to be free
Like catching tadpoles and climbing a tree

We played with a whip and top
Waiting for the first one to stop
We would be over the woods getting bluebells
Or down the beach making sandcastles and collecting shells

Far away from the shows our parents would take us
As we had just enough money for the bus
But they were happy days
And we made our fun in simple ways.

June Newell

STAIRWAY TO HEAVEN

If there was a stairway to Heaven
Then I would take a chance
I'd climb each step with memories
To treasure one more glance
To see the smile upon your face
To hold your big, rough hand
To walk with you
And talk to you
Throughout the promised land
I've never found that stairway
But I'm looking all the time
Maybe one day in a dream
I will have the chance
To take a peek into your world
And treasure one more glance.

Deena Howard